BATTLES INVOLVING THAILAND

Books LLC®, Reference Series, Memphis, USA, 2011. www.booksllc.net. Copyright: http://creativecommons.org/licenses/by-sa/3.0/deed.en

Table of Contents

Battles involving Thailand
Battle of Prachuab Khirikhan............. 1
Battle of Rạch Gầm-Xoài Mút............ 2
Nine Army Battle................................. 3
Ta Din Dang campaign 3

Battles of the Franco-Siamese War

Paknam incident.................................. 3

Battles of the Franco-Thai War
Battle of Koh Chang 4

Battles of the Korean War involving Thailand

Third Battle of Seoul........................... 6

Battles of the Vietnam War involving Thailand
Battle of Hat Dich 11
Battle of Lima Site 85 24

Introduction

Purchase of this book entitles you to a free trial membership in the publisher's book club at www.booksllc.net. (Time limited offer.) Simply enter the barcode number from the back cover onto the membership form. The book club entitles you to select from hundreds of thousands of books at no additional charge. You can also download a digital copy of this and related books to read on the go. Simply enter the title or subject onto the search form to find them.

Each chapter in this book ends with a URL to a hyperlinked online version. Type the URL exactly as it appears. If you change the URL's capitalization it won't work. Use the online version to access related pages, websites, footnotes, tables, color photos, updates. Click the version history tab to see the chapter's contributors. Click the edit link to suggest changes.

A large and diverse editor base collaboratively wrote the book, not a single author. After a long process of discussion and debate, the chapters gradually took on a neutral point of view reached through consensus. Additional editors expanded and contributed to chapters striving to achieve balance and comprehensive coverage. This reduced the regional or cultural bias found in many other books and provided access and breadth on subject matter otherwise little documented.

Battle of Prachuab Khirikhan

The **Battle of Prachuab Khrikhan** was an early engagement of the Japanese Invasion of Thailand in the South-East Asian Theatre of World War II. It was fought on December 8, 1941 at the airfield of Prachuap Khiri Khan in Thailand, on the coast of the Gulf of Thailand along the Kra Isthmus. The Japanese meant to use Thailand as a base to strike at British possessions in Burma and Malaya and attacked Thailand without warning.

Battle

Fighting took place at *Ao Manao* beach

At about 03:00 on December 8, 1941, the 2nd Battalion, 143rd Infantry Regiment, 55th Division of the Imperial Japanese Army, under the command of Major Kisoyoshi Utsunomiya, began landing troops at Prachuab Khiri Khan. When informed of invasion, Wing Commander M. L. Prawat Chumsai of *Kong Bin Noi* (Squadron) 5 immediately gave orders to resist. The units on the airfield were equipped with six heavy and two light machine guns, which they immediately turned against the Japanese troops trying to surround the airfield. The small garrison of pilots and ground crew was reinforced by members of the constabulary and Yuwachon Thaharn (a quasi-military teenage auxiliary) who had managed to escape from the town of Prachuab Khiri Khan after the Japanese had captured the telegraph office and the police station.

Despite the fact that the Japanese had occupied part of the airfield, *Kong Bin Noi* 5's pilots attempted to take off at sunrise to bomb and strafe the advancing Japanese.

Chief Warrant Officer Prom Chuwong was first to take off in a Hawk III. However, Japanese ground fire quickly shot him down, killing him. The Japanese shot down two more Hawks as they attempted to take off, killing both pilots, and wounded a third pilot as he brought his Hawk onto the runway. Only one other pilot managed to get airborne. Flying Officer Man Prasongdi took off in a Hawk III armed with four 50 kg bombs and attempted to attack Japanese transports in Manao harbour. However, he could not locate them due to heavy fog and rain.

By 08:00, most of the northern hangars were in Japanese hands. The Thais smashed the instruments of the isolated airfield control tower and set fire to it, as the runways were abandoned. A new perimeter was set up and the withdrawing airmen were covered by a machine gun positioned in the clubhouse's tennis court, manned by Airmen Singto Saensukh and Kasem Wongkangya. The machine gun kept firing throughout the morning and into the afternoon.

Pilot Officer Somsri Suchrittham and his men, whose strength was now around thirty, were forced to withdraw when their northern flank was threatened by the abandonment of the runways.

Having successfully secured the beachhead, the Japanese proceeded to occupy what was left of the hangars and runways, and reinforcements -- including artillery and ten tanks -- were landed from the transports.

The families of the airmen took refuge in the guesthouses on Mount Laum Muak. The evacuation of the living quarters was supervised by Pilot Officer Phol Thongpricha.

Another position was set up by defenders, who divided themselves into three groups. One group was stationed by the guest houses on Prachuab Bay and fired on anything coming up the road from the guard house.

A second group, under the immediate command of Wing Commander Prawat, placed itself in the area around the Command and administrative buildings. The final group occupied in houses facing Manao Bay. These two groups fired on the approaches from the hangars and the runways.

Fighting continued into late evening, but with lessening intensity. The machine gun at the tennis court held back the Japanese, while a light machine gun was held in reserve and moved to plug any gaps in the perimeter.

Rumours that Royal Thai Navy sailors were fighting their way through to relieve the airmen kept up Thai hopes through the night. Ammunition was low, and at one point the airmen actually fired blank rounds at the Japanese.

The following morning, the exhausted Thais received a telegram from the Ministry of the Interior, brought in by a postman during a lull in the battle. The telegram ordered the defenders to cease fighting, as an armistice had been arranged by the government.

However, the Thais felt this was a trick by the Japanese and continued to resist. The infuriated invaders now mounted assaults with renewed vigour. The defenders were slowly pushed back. About this time, the lone machine gun in the tennis court was taken out, both gunners severely wounded.

By 10:00, with the Japanese closing in, Wing Commander Prawat ordered the Command Building to be burned, along with all military documents. As flames engulfed the building, Flying Officer Prayad Kanchonwiroj, the senior medical officer, ordered the hospital building evacuated and set on fire.

Wing Commander Prawat ordered all officers to save a bullet for themselves and said that those who wished to were free to try to break out on their own. The others, including the wounded, were to fall back on Mount Laum Muak.

At noon, a civilian car with a small white flag arrived. It contained a number of Thai government officials, including the province's undersecretary, Jarunphan Isarangun na Ayutthaya. Jarunphan handed Wing Commander Prawat a direct order from the prime minister, Field Marshal Phibunsongkhram, telling him to cease resistance immediately. Fighting officially ended at 12:35 am on December 8, 1941.

Losses

The Thais suffered 38 dead and 27 wounded, including airmen, police and civilians. Wing Commander Prawat's pregnant wife was among the dead, killed by a stray bullet. Japanese sources stated that the Japanese suffered 115 dead. However, Thai estimates of Japanese losses were put at 217 dead and more than 300 wounded.

Source (edited): "http://en.wikipedia.org/wiki/Battle_of_Prachuab_Khirikhan"

Battle of Rạch Gầm-Xoài Mút

The **Battle of Rạch Gầm-Xoài Mút** was fought between Tây-Sơn (Vietnamese) and Siamese forces in present-day Tiền Giang Province on January 19, 1785. It went down as one of the greatest victories in Vietnamese history.

Background

In 1783 when Tây-Sơn rebel forces recaptured Saigon and forced Nguyễn Ánh to escape across the river to Siam. While in exile Nguyễn Ánh wished to retake Gia Định and push the Tây-Sơn rebels out. One of Anh's general, Chau Van Tiep, convinced the peaceful King Buddha Yodfa Chulaloke of Siam to provide Nguyen Anh with support troops and a small invasion force.

In mid-1784 Nguyễn Ánh, with 20,000-50,000 Siamese troops and 300 warships, moved through Cambodia, then East of Tonle Sap (Toh Lay Sap in Thai) and penetrated the recently annexed provinces of Annam. 20,000 Siamese troops reached Kiên Giang and another 30,000 landed in Chap Lap, as the Siamese advanced towards Cần Thơ. Later that year the Siamese captured the former Cambodian province of Gia Định where, they committed atrocities against the population of Việt settlers, this made some locals turn their support into Tây Sơn.

Battle

The Tay Son reforcements led by

Nguyen Hue marched south from Quy Nhon and arrived Cochin China territory soon after. Hue avoided a direct attack into strong Siamese force at Sa Dec and tried to setup a trap. Nguyễn Huệ, anticipating a move from the Siamese, had secretly positioned his infantry and artillery along the Mekong River (Rạch Gầm-Xoài Mút area of present day Tiền Giang province), and on some islands in the middle, facing other troops on the northern banks with naval reinforcements on both sides of the infantry positions.

On the morning of January 20, 1785 Nguyễn Huệ sent a small naval force, under a banner of truce, to lure the Siamese into his trap. After so many victories, the Siamese army and naval forces were overconfident. So, they went to the parley, unaware of the trap.

Nguyễn Huệ's ships dashed into the unprepared Siamese troops, prevented them from advance or retreat. In the meanwhile, Tay Son artillery opened firing. The battle ended with a near annihilation of the Siamese force, Vietnamese source recorded that all the ships of the Siamese navy were destroyed and only 2,000-3,000 of the original expedition survived to escape back across the river into Siam. Nguyen Anh and his family members escaped and later went to Siam.

Gallery

Weapons remained after the battle

Vietnamese monument of the batlle
Source (edited): "http://en.wikipedia.org/wiki/Battle_of_R%E1%BA%A1ch_G%E1%BA%A7m-Xo%C3%A0i_M%C3%BAt"

Nine Army Battle

The **Nine-Army Battle** (1795) is the name given to the defense of the Thai Kingdom by Buddha Yodfa Chulaloke against an invasion by King Bodawpaya of Burma. Today it is commemorated by a park, established by the Royal Thai Army, 40 kilometres (25 mi) from the town of Kanchanaburi.

The Nine Army Battle is famous within Thailand and remembered as one of the great victories for the country. There were 144,000 Burmese foot-soldiers and cavalry facing only 70,000 Thai soldiers.

Source (edited): "http://en.wikipedia.org/wiki/Nine_Army_Battle"

Ta Din Dang campaign

"Ta Din Dang campaign" was a short conflict, occurring in 1786. As his armies were destroyed, Bodawpaya retreated, only to renew attacks next year . Bodawpaya, this time, did not divide his troops but instead formed into single army. Bodawpaya passed through the Chedi Sam Ong and settled in Ta Din Dang. The Front Palace marched the Siamese forces to face Bodawpaya. The fighting was very short and Bodawpaya was quickly defeated.

Source (edited): "http://en.wikipedia.org/wiki/Ta_Din_Dang_campaign"

Paknam incident

The **Paknam Incident** was a military engagement fought during the Franco-Siamese War in July 1893. While sailing off Paknam through Siam's Chao Phraya River, three French ships were fired on by a Siamese fort and force of gunboats. In the ensuing battle, France won and proceeded to blockade Bangkok which ended the war.

Background

Conflict arose when the French Navy aviso *Inconstant* and the gunboat *Comete* arrived at Paknam and requested permission to cross the bar into the Chao Phraya. The French were on their way to Bankok, further up the river, for negotiations. When the Siamese refused, the French commander Rear Admiral Edgar Humann disregarded the Siamese demands and instructions from his own government. Before the action, Rear Admiral Humann had been ordered not to cross the bar because the Siamese were well prepared for battle. Siamese forces included the recently built Chulachomklao Fort with seven 6-inch disappearing guns. The Siamese also sunk several junks and a cargo ship in the river, creating only one narrow passage which the French had to exploit.

Five gunboats were anchored just beyond the sunken junks, they were the *Makut Ratchakuman*, *Narubent Butri*, *Thun Kramon*, *Muratha Wisitsawat* and the *Han Hak*. Two were modern warships while the others were older gunboats or converted river steamers. A sea mine field of sixteen explosives was also laid. Many Europeans served in the Siamese military at this time, a Dutch admiral commanded the fort while Vice Admiral Phraya Chonlayut Yothin commanded the gunboats.

Incident

A gun of Chulachomklao Fort firing on the French ships.

The French chose to cross the bar just after sunset on July 13, their objective was to fight there way past the Siamese defenses but only if fired upon. The weather was overcast. By this time the Siamese were on high alert and at battle stations. The French ships were towed into action by the small mail steamer *Jean Baptiste Say*. At 6:15 pm the rain stopped and the Siamese gunners observed the French ships passing the nearby lighthouse. A few minutes later, the French were off Black Buoy when they entered the range of the fort. Siamese gunners were ordered to fire three warning shots, if they were ignored, then a fourth would signal their gunboats to begin firing.

At 6:30, the fort opened fire with two blank rounds but the French continued on so a third, live, warning shot was fired and hit the water in front of the *Jean Baptiste Say*. When this warning was ignored a fourth shot was fired so the gunboats *Makhut Ratchakuman* and *Muratha Wasitsawat* opened up at 6:50. *Inconstant* returned fired on the fort while the *Comete* engaged the gunboats. A small boat filled with explosives was also sent out to ram one of the French ships but it missed its target. Combat lasted about twenty-five minutes.

Ultimately Rear Admiral Humann forced his way through the Siamese line, ramming and sinking one gunboat in the process. One other was hit by shell fire, ten men were killed and twelve others wounded. The French suffered as well, while towing the warships past Paknam, the *Jean Baptiste Say* was hit several times by cannon fire. Her commander was forced to cut the tow line and ground his ship on Laem Lamphu Rai while the *Inconstant* and *Comete* proceeded onto Bangkok. Three Frenchmen were killed and two others were wounded. *Comete* received more hits than the *Inconstant* but the damage was not serious. The Siamese fort was not damaged.

Aftermath

The following morning, *Jean Baptiste Say*'s crew was still on board their grounded vessel so the Siamese sent a boat and captured the steamer, they then attempted and failed to sink her. The prisoners were treated badly according to reports and put in a Bankok prison. A day later, the French gunboat *Forfait* arrived at Paknam and sent a boat full of sailors to recapture the mail steamer but when they boarded, the Siamese occupants successfully repelled the attack. When Rear Admiral Humann arrived off Bankok, he established a blockade, trainned his guns on the royal palace and on October 3, 1893, a treaty was signed, ending the war.

Source (edited): "http://en.wikipedia.org/wiki/Paknam_incident"

Battle of Koh Chang

The **Battle of Koh Chang** took place on 17 January 1941 during the French-Thai War and resulted in a decisive victory by the French over the Royal Thai Navy. During the battle, a flotilla a French warships attacked a smaller force of Thai vessels, including a coastal battleship.

In the end, Thailand lost two ships sunk and one heavily damaged and grounded. Within a month of the engagement, the Vichy French and the Thais negotiated a peace which ended the war.

Background

Thai Navy

The Royal Thai Navy had been modernized with the recent acquisition of vessels from Japan and Italy. The major units of the fleet included two Japanese-built armoured coast defence vessels, which displaced 2,500 long tons (2,500 t) and carried 8 in (200 mm) guns, two older British-built armoured gunboats with 6 in (150 mm) guns, 12 torpedo boats and four submarines.

In addition, the Royal Thai Air Force had in its inventory over 140 aircraft, including relatively modern Mitsubishi Ki-30 light bombers, which saw extensive service against the French. These aircraft in themselves were quite capable of causing severe damage to any French naval mission which might be mounted. Other less capable aircraft in the Thai inventory included P-36 Hawk fighters, 70 Chance-Vought O2U-2 Corsair biplanes, six Martin B-10 bombers and several Avro 504 trainers.

French Navy

Lamotte-Piquet.

Despite the strengths of the Thai forces the French Governor General of Indochina and Commander-in-Chief Naval Forces, Admiral Jean Decoux, decided that the naval mission should go ahead. A small squadron, the Groupe Occasionnel, was formed on 9 December 1940 at Cam Ranh Bay, near Saigon, under the command of *Capitaine de Vaisseau* Régis Bérenger.

The squadron consisted of the light cruiser *Lamotte-Piquet*, the avisos Dumont d'Urville *PG 77* (2) and Amiral Charner *PG 81* (2), and the older avisos *Tahure* and *Marne*. There was no air cover to speak of, apart from eight Loire 130 seaplanes based at Ream which provided reconnaissance. Additional scouting was provided by three coastal survey craft, and intelligence gleaned from the local fishermen.

Bérenger's squadron began training manoeuvres in Cam Ranh Bay shortly after coming together. Early in the new year, on 13 January 1941, Admiral Decoux formally requested Bérenger to send the squadron against the Thais to act in support of a land offensive planned for 16 January. This operation was intended to throw back Thai forces which had been advancing along the coast. Because of the disparate speeds of the French ships, Bérenger sent the slower sloops on ahead, while he remained in Saigon to complete the final elements of the plan.

Several options were currently being prepared, the Admiralty in Paris having recently given its formal blessing to the use of naval forces in support of the army. The final planning meeting of the 13th saw an immediate delay in the execution of the operation for 24 hours. With the plans finalised, Bérenger sailed in *Lamotte-Picquet*, the delay in the start of the operation allowing him to refuel at Cap St. Jacques before the rendezvous with the slower ships at 16:00 on the 15th, 20 mi (17 nmi; 32 km) North of Poulo Condore.

The orders from Admiral Decoux were clear and simple, "attack the Siamese coastal city from Rayong to the Cambodian frontier to force Siamese government to retreat the arms force from Cambodian frontier". On the evening of the 15th, following a final conference on board the flagship, the squadron weighed anchor at 21:15 and closed the Thai coast at 14 kn (16 mph; 26 km/h), the best speed of the sloops. The French ships remained undetected as they entered the Gulf of Siam, but their quarry was not so lucky. The Loire 130s from Ream had completed a sweep of the coast from Trat to Sattahib. They had located one coast defence ship and two torpedo boats at Koh Chang, and one gunboat, four torpedo boats and two submarines at Satahib.

Their report was sent to Marine Headquarters in Saigon, who retransmitted the report to *Lamotte-Picquet*. Bérenger considered his options in the light of this intelligence and opted for a dawn attack on Koh Chang. He discounted an attack on Sattahib because it was not possible for the sloops to reach the port until later in the day, by which time the Thai force was likely to have been alerted to the French presence and the element of surprise would be lost. In addition, there was doubt as to the contribution which the harbour defences at Satahib could make. Finally, the force at Koh Chang, although formidable, was the weaker of the two and was thought to offer the best chance for victory.

Bérenger's plan of attack was as follows. The squadron would approach at dawn from the South West. Because the anchorage at Koh Chang was surrounded by islands and islets, many of which were over 200 metres high, the squadron would break up and use the cover of the islands to concentrate fire on portions of the Thai squadron whilst covering all the avenues of escape. The easternmost channel was regarded as the most likely route by which a breakout would be made — this was the most suitable route and was also the area in which the recce report had placed the largest Thai ships. *Lamotte-Picquet* would head to the eastern side of the anchorage to block this route whilst the colonial sloops blocked the centre and pounded the Thai ships there. The smaller French ships would concentrate to the West.

Battle

Amiral Charner

The French squadron closed on the anchorage at 05:30 on 17 January. At 05:45, they split into the three groups as planned, *Lamotte-Picquet* heading for the eastern part of the anchorage, *Dumont d'Urville* and *Amiral Charner* continuing to the central position and *Tahure* and *Marne* heading for the western side. Conditions were perfect — the weather was fine, the seas calm and almost flat. Sunrise was due at 06:30, and the scene was lit only by the first rays of light on the horizon and by the dim moonlight.

A final aerial reconnaissance of the target area had been arranged using one of the Ream-based Loire 130s. *Lamotte-Picquet* carried two such aircraft, but these could not be launched due to catapult problems. At 06:05, the Loire 130 overflew the anchorage and reported two torpedo ships. This came as a nasty surprise to the French — previous reports led them to believe that only one of the torpedo boat was present, but during the night, HTMS *Chonburi* had arrived to relieve *Chantaburi*, which was to return to Satahib later that day for repairing.

Once their presence had been passed to *Lamotte-Picquet* the aircraft attempted an attack of its own using bombs, but was forced off by a heavy barrage of AA fire. The effect of this mission was double edged — the French were now aware that they faced both the Thai units, but the element of surprise had been wasted and there was still thirty minutes to go until sunrise. Caught napping by the oncoming French the Thais desperately began to raise steam and prepared to slip their anchors, but the torpedo boats were sunk by gunfire from *Lamotte-Picquet*.

At 06:38, the lookouts in *Lamotte-Picquet* spotted the coastal defence ship HTMS *Thonburi*, heading northwest, at a range of 10,000 metres (11,000 yd). A running battle ensued, with the fire of both ships frequently blocked by the towering islets. The fire from the Thai ship was heavy, but inaccurate. By 07:15, fires could be seen on *Thonburi*, which then found herself engaged not only by the cruiser but also by the sloops. In the beginning of the engagement, a lucky shot from *Lamotte-Picquet* killed the captain of *Thonburi*, Commander Luang Phrom Viraphan, and disrupted her operations. Believing they had a better chance of hurting the smaller French ships the Thais shifted their fire onto *Admiral Charner*, which soon found 8 in (200 mm) salvoes falling around her.

Thonburi shifted fire back to *Lamotte-Picquet* after a salvo from the French cruiser put her after turret out of action. Soon she reached the safety of shallow water which the French ships could not enter for fear of grounding, but it all came too late for the hapless Thais as *Thonburi* was burning fiercely and listing heavily to starboard. Her remaining turret was manned and hand and could not fire unless the maneuvers of the ship put it in appropriate position. At 07:50, *Lamotte-Picquet* fired a final salvo of torpedoes at 15,000 metres (16,000 yd), but lost sight of *Thonburi* behind an island from which she was not seen to emerge.

For the next hour, the French ships patrolled the area, picking up survivors and ensuring their victory was total. At 08:40, Bérenger ordered the squadron to head for home, but this coincided with the start of the expected Thai air attacks. Thai planes dropped several bombs close to *Lamotte-Picquet* and scored one hit, although the bomb failed to explode. *Lamotte-Picquet*'s anti-aircraft guns put up a vigorous barrage and further attacks were not pressed home. The final raid departed at 09:40, after which the victorious French squadron returned to Saigon.

Aftermath

A plaque commemorating the battle.

The French left behind them a scene of total devastation. *Thonburi* was heavily damaged and grounded on a sand bar in the mouth of the Chantaboun river, with about 20 dead. She was later raised and repaired by the Japanese, survived the war and was used as a training ship until she was retired. The Thai transport HTMS *Chang* arrived at Koh Chang shortly after the French departed and took *Thonburi* in tow.

The torpedo boat *Chonburi* was sunk with a loss of two men and HTMS *Songhkla* also sank with a loss of fourteen dead. The only survivors were rescued by the torpedo boat HTMS *Rayong*, the minelayer HTMS *Nhong Sarhai* and the fishery protection vessel *Thiew Uthok*. These three ships, which had been sheltering to the north of Koh Chang, wisely chose not to break cover and thus were not observed by the French. The French were elated, for they had inflicted a defeat as decisive in its way as the Japanese at Tsushima.

Their success is all the more notable when the difficulties of navigating and fighting in such confined waters are considered, and given the courage and tenacity which the Thai sailors exhibited during the action, a fact which the French were gracious to accept. In the end, though, it was all for nought — five days later the Japanese government offered to arbitrate in the search for a peaceful settlement, and soon confirmed the Thai annexations. Even this state of affairs did not last for long, as Thailand was invaded later that year during the attacks on Malaya, and was forced to return her short-lived gains to France at the end of World War II.

Thonburi was later raised by Royal Thai Navy. She was repaired in Japan and was used as a training ship until she was decommissioned. Her gun and deck are placed as a memorial in the Royal Thai Naval Academy, Samut Prakan.

During the post-action investigations, it was claimed, on the evidence of sailors and the fisherman around Koh Chang, heavy damage was seen to have been caused to *Lamotte-Picquet* and her fleet. The report claims the crew of *Lamotte-Picquet* spent all of the following night repairing the damage.

Source (edited): "http://en.wikipedia.org/wiki/Battle_of_Koh_Chang"

Third Battle of Seoul

The **Third Battle of Seoul**, also known as the **Chinese New Year's Offensive**, the **January–Fourth Retreat** (Korean: 1·4 후퇴) or the **Third Phase Campaign Western Sector** (simplified Chinese: 第三次战役西线; pinyin: *Dì Sān Cì Zhàn Yī Xī Xiàn*), was a battle of the Korean War, which took place from December 31, 1950 to January 7, 1951 around the South Korean capital of Seoul. In the aftermath of the major Chinese victory at the Battle of the Ch'ongch'on River, the United Nations Command started to contemplate on the possibility of evacuation from the Korean Peninsula. Upon learning this development, China's Chairman Mao Zedong ordered the Chinese People's Volunteer Army to cross the 38th parallel in an effort to pressure the United Nations forces to withdraw from South Korea.

On the New Year Eve of 1951, the Chinese 13th Army attacked the Republic of Korea (ROK) 1st, 2nd, 5th and 6th Infantry Divisions along the 38th parallel, breaching United Nations Forces' defenses at the Imjin River, Hantan River, Gapyeong and Chuncheon in the process. To prevent the Chinese forces from overwhelming the defenders, the United States Eighth Army under the command of Lieutenant General Matthew B. Ridgway evacuated Seoul on January 3, 1951.

Although Chinese forces captured Seoul by the end of the battle, the Chinese invasion of South Korea galvanized the United Nations' support for South Korea, while the idea of evacuation was soon abandoned by the United Nations Command. At the same time, the Chinese People's Volunteer Army were completely exhausted after months of nonstop fighting since the start of the Chinese intervention, thereby allowing the United Nations forces to regain the initiative in Korea.

Background

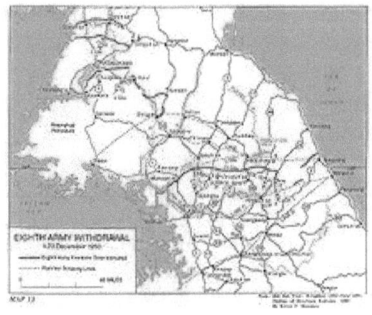

Map of US Eighth Army retreat, December 1 – 23, 1950.

With the People's Republic of China entering the Korean War during the winter of 1950, the Korean War had entered a new phase. To prevent North Korea from falling under United Nations (UN) control after the UN landing at Incheon, the Chinese People's Volunteer Army (PVA) entered Korea and launched a series of surprise attacks against the UN forces near the Sino-Korean border at the end of 1950. The resulting battles at the Ch'ongch'on River Valley and the Chosin Reservoir forced the UN forces to retreat back to the 38th parallel by December 1950, with Chinese and North Korean forces recapturing much of North Korea. On the Korean western front, after the United States Eighth Army suffered a disastrous defeat at the Ch'ongch'on River, the Eighth Army retreated back to the Imjin River while setting up defensive positions around the South Korean capital of Seoul. Although the US Eighth Army was ordered to hold Seoul for as long as possible, General Douglas MacArthur planned a series of withdrawals to the Pusan Perimeter under the assumption that UN forces were about to be overwhelmed in Korea. General Walton Walker, commander of the US Eighth Army, was killed in a traffic accident on December 23, and Lieutenant General Matthew B. Ridgway assumed command of the Eighth Army on December 26, 1950. At the UN, a ceasefire along the 38th parallel was proposed to China on December 11, 1950 in order to avoid any further escalation of hostility between China and US.

Although the Chinese People's Volunteer Army had been weakened from their earlier battles, with nearly 40 percent of its forces rendered combat ineffective, its unexpected victories over the UN forces had convinced the Chinese leadership in the invincibility of PVA. Immediately after the PVA 13th Army's victory over the US Eighth Army at the Ch'ongch'on River, China's Chairman Mao Zedong started to contemplate another offensive against the UN forces on the urging of North Korean Premier Kim Il-sung. After learning of MacArthur's plans and the UN ceasefire, Mao also believed that the UN evacuation of the Korean Peninsula was imminent. Although the over-stretched Chinese logistics prevented the PVA from launching a full scale invasion against South Korea, Mao still ordered the PVA 13th Army to launch an intrusion, dubbed the "Third Phase Campaign", to hasten the UN withdrawal and to demonstrate China's desire for a total victory in Korea. On December 23, 1950, China's Foreign Minister Zhou Enlai formally rejected the UN ceasefire while demanding all UN forces to be withdrawn from the Korean Peninsula.

Prelude

Locations, terrain and weather

Seoul is the capital city of South Korea, which is roughly bisected into northern and southern halves by the Han River. Seoul is also located at 35 mi (56 km) south of the 38th parallel. The battle was fought over the UN defenses at the 38th parallel, which stretches horizontally from the Imjin River mouth on the Korean west coast to the town of Chuncheon in central Korea. A road dubbed "Route 33" runs south across the 38th parallel at the Hantan River, passes through Uijeongbu and eventually arrives at Seoul, and it is an ancient invasion route towards Seoul. Another road ran across the Imjin River, and it connects Seoul and Kaesong through the town of Munsan and Koyang. Finally, a road runs through Chuncheon and it connects to Seoul from the northeast. The harsh Korean winter, with temperatures as low as −20 °C (−4 °F), had frozen the Imjin and the Hantan River over most of the river crossings, and it eliminated a major obstacle for the attacking Chinese forces.

By December 22, 1950, the US Eighth Army's front had stabilized along the 38th parallel. Just days before his death, Walker placed the US I Corps, the US IX Corps, and the ROK III Corps of the Eighth Army along the 38th parallel to defend Seoul. The US I and IX Corps were to defend the Imjin and Hantan River respectively, while the ROK III Corps were to guard the areas around Chuncheon. The boundary between US I and IX Corps was marked by Route 33, and it is defended by the ROK 1st Infantry Division on the west side and the ROK 6th Infantry Division on the east side.

Because the South Korean forces had suffered nearly 45,000 casualties at the end of 1950, most of the South Korean units were composed of raw recruits with little combat training. After inspecting the front just days before the battle, General J. Lawton Collins, the US Army Chief of Staff, concluded that most of the ROK formations were only fit for outpost duties. At the same time, the US Eighth Army was also suffering from low morale due to its earlier defeats, and most of its soldiers were anticipating an evacuation from Korea. The Eight Army's lack of will to fight and to maintain contact with Chinese forces resulted in a lack of information on Chinese troop movements and intentions. After inspecting the front on December 27, Ridgway ordered the US I and IX Corps to organize a new defensive line around Koyang to Uijeongbu, called the Seoul Bridgehead line, to cover the Han River crossings in case the UN forces were forced to evacuate Seoul.

The Chinese forces, however, were also suffering from logistics problems and exhaustion from their earlier victories. Arguing against the Third Phase Campaign on December 7, PVA Commander Peng Dehuai telegraphed to Mao that the PVA would need at least three months to replace its casualties, while most of its troops were in critical need of resupply, rest and reorganization. The Chinese logistics system, which was based on the concept of People's War with the native population supplying the army, also ran into difficulties due to the indifferent, and sometimes hostile, Korean population near the 38th parallel. The Chinese were now suffering from hunger and the lack of winter clothing.

Responding to Peng's concern over the troops' conditions, Mao limited the scope of the Third Phase Campaign to pin down the South Korean forces along the 38th parallel while inflicting as much damage as possible. Upon noticing that the US units were not interspersed between the South Korean formations, therefore unable to support the South Koreans, Mao ordered the PVA 13th Army to destroy the ROK 1st Infantry Division, the ROK 6th Infantry Division and the ROK III Corps. Following Mao's instruction, Peng placed the PVA 38th, 39th, 40th and 50th Corps of the 13th Army in front of the ROK 1st and 6th Infantry Division, while the 42nd and the 66th Corps of the 13th Army were moved into ROK III Corps' sector. The start date of the offensive was set to the New Year's Eve in order to take advantage of the night assault under a full moon and the low alertness of the UN soldiers during the holiday, and Ridgway had also predicted that the New Year Eve would be the likely time for the new Chinese offensive. Believing that the destruction of the South Koreans forces at the 38th parallel would render the UN forces incapable of counterattacks in the future, Mao promised to pull all Chinese troops off the front line for rest and refit by the end of the campaign.

Battle

On the evening of December 31, 1950, the PVA 13th Army launched a massive attack against South Korean forces along the 38th parallel. Along the Imjin River and the Hantan River, the PVA 38th, 39th, 40th and 50th Corps managed to decimate the ROK 1st Division while routing the ROK 6th Division. At the Chuncheon sector, the PVA 42nd and the 66th Corps forced the ROK III Corps into full retreat. With the defenses at the 38th parallel completely collapsed by January 1, 1951, Ridgway ordered the evacuation of Seoul on January 3.

Actions at the Imjin River and the Hantan River

Map of the Chinese Third Phase Campaign.

By December 15, 1950, the ROK 1st Infantry Division had retreated back to the town of Choksong on the southern bank of the Imjin River—its original defensive position at the start of the Korean War. On the right flank of the ROK 1st Infantry Division, the ROK 6th Infantry Division was located at the north of Tongduch'on along the southern bank of the Hantan River. The ROK 1st Infantry Division planned to defend the Imjin River by placing its 11th and 12th Regiments at the west and the east side of Choksong respectively, while the ROK 6th Infantry Division defended the Route 33 at the Hantan River by placing its 7th and 19th Regiments on each side of the road. Both the ROK 15th Regiment of the 1st Infantry Division and the ROK 2nd Regiment of the 6th Infantry Division were placed in the rear as reserves. The South Koreans had also constructed numerous bunkers, barbed wire obstacles and minefields on both banks of the river in order to strengthen defenses and to maintain troop morale.

Faced with the South Korean defense, the Chinese prepared for well over a month for the upcoming offensive. In the weeks before the operational orders for the Third Phase Campaign were issued by PVA High Command, the advance elements of the PVA 39th Corps had been conducting detailed reconnaissance on South Korean defenses. The South Korean positions were then thoroughly analyzed by Chinese commanders, engineers and artillery officers. Chinese "thrust" companies, which were composed of specially trained assault and engineer teams, were also organized to lead the attack across the Imjin and Hantan River. Although during the preparation, the Chinese artillery units had suffered heavy losses under UN air attacks, PVA Deputy Commander Han Xianchu still managed to bring up 100 artillery pieces against the South Korean fortifications. On December 22, the PVA High Command issued the operational orders that signaled the start of the Third Phase Campaign. The PVA 39th and 50th Corps were tasked with the destruction of the ROK 1st Infantry Division, while the 38th and the 40th Corps were tasked with the destruction of the ROK 6th Infantry Division.

Acting on Ridgway's prediction, the ROK Army Headquarters ordered all units to full alert at the dusk of December 31, but many of its soldiers were either drunk from the New Year celebration or abandoned their posts in order to escape the cold. The Chinese artillery units began to bomb the South Korean defenses at 1630 on December 31. The first blow fell on the ROK 12th Regiment of the 1st Infantry Division, due to the fact that it acted as both the boundary between the ROK 1st and 6th Infantry Divisions and the boundary between US I and IX Corps. Because the river banks on ROK 12th Regiment's flanks were composed of high cliffs difficult for the attackers to scale, most of the regiment's strength were used to defend its center. Upon noticing this development, the PVA 39th Corps decided to use ROK 12th Regiment's flanks as the main points of attack in order to achieve maximum surprise. Following a feint attack on the ROK 12th Regiment's center, the PVA 116th and the 117th Divisions of the 38th Corps struck both flanks of the ROK 12th Regiment. The ROK 12th Regiment was caught off guard and offered little resistance, and within hours the regiment was cut to pieces with a battery of the US 9th Field Artillery Battalion seized by the Chinese. Under the cover of the fleeing Korean soldiers, the attacking Chinese forces then penetrated the ROK 15th Regiment's defense without firing a shot. Desperate to contain the Chinese breakthrough, Brigadier General Paik Sun Yup of the ROK 1st Infantry Division used the division's rear service personnel to form an assault battalion, but the battalion was unable to stop the Chinese advance. With only the ROK 11th Regiment remaining intact by the morning of January 1, the ROK 1st Infantry Division was forced to withdraw on January 2.

The Chinese attacks against the ROK 6th Infantry Division, however, did not go as commanders had planned. The original plan called for the PVA 38th and the 40th Corps to attack the ROK 19th Regiment on the 6th Infantry Division's right flank, but the bulk of the Chinese forces mistakenly attacked the US 19th Infantry Regiment of the US 24th Infantry Division, which was stationed to the east of the ROK 19th Regiment. The poor intelligence had also made the Chinese charge through several minefields, resulting in heavy casualties to the attackers. But with no regards to the losses, the Chinese pushed the US 19th Infantry Regiment back, exposing the right flank of the ROK 6th Infantry Division in the process. With the ROK 1st Infantry Division out of action and the US 24th Infantry Division's defenses penetrated, the Chinese forces on both flanks of the ROK 6th Infantry Division then advanced southward in order to encircle the division. By midnight of the New Year's Eve, the ROK 6th Infantry Division was forced into full retreat. Although the Chinese managed to intercept some elements of the ROK 6th Infantry Division, most of the South Koreans escaped the trap by infiltrating the Chinese lines using the mountain trails. As Ridgway tried to inspect the front on the morning of January 1, he was greeted by the fleeing and weaponless remnants of the ROK 6th Infantry Division a few miles north of Seoul. But despite Ridgway's efforts to stop the retreat, the division continued to flee south. It was not until the personal intervention of South Korean President Syngman Rhee that the division finally stopped its retreat. By the night of January 1, the UN defenses at the Imjin River and the Hantan River had completely collapsed with the Chinese advancing 9 mi (14 km) into UN territory. The Chinese stopped their advance on January 2.

Actions at Gapyeong and Chuncheon

The ROK III Corps, which was located to the east of the US 24th Infantry Division of the US IX Corps, defended the 38th parallel to the north of Gapyeong (Kapyong) and Chuncheon. Composed of four divisions, the ROK III Corps placed its ROK 2nd Infantry Division on the corps' left flank at the hills north of Gapyeong, while the ROK 5th Infantry Division defended the corps' center at Chuncheon. The cold winter created great difficulties for the South Korean defenders, with the heavy snow hindering construction and icy roads limiting food and ammunition supplies. North Korean guerrillas were also active in the region, and had caused serious disruption in the rear of the ROK III Corps.

The Chinese operational order for the Third Phase Campaign called for the 42nd and the 66th Corps to protect the Chinese left flank by eliminating the ROK 2nd and 5th Infantry Divisions, while cutting the road between Chuncheon and Seoul. Following instructions, the two Chinese corps quickly struck after midnight on New Year's Eve. The PVA 124th Division first penetrated the flanks of the ROK 2nd Infantry Division, then blocked the division's retreat route. The trapped ROK 17th and 32nd Regiments of the ROK 2nd Infantry Division were forced to retreat in disarray. With the PVA 66th Corps pressuring the ROK 5th Infantry Division's front, the PVA 124th Division then advanced eastward in the Korean rear and blocked the ROK 5th Infantry Division's retreat route as well. The maneuver soon left the ROK 36th Regiment of the ROK 5th Infantry Division surrounded by Chinese, and the ROK 36th Regiment had to escape by infiltrating the Chinese lines using mountain trails. By January 1, the ROK III Corps had lost contact with the 2nd and 5th Infantry Divisions, while the rest of the III Corps were retreating to the town of Wonju. On January 5, the PVA 42nd and 66th Corps were relieved by the North Korean People's Army (KPA) II and V Corps, and the North Koreans launched a separate offensive towards Wonju.

Evacuation of Seoul

A knocked out Cromwell tank of the Cooper Force.

In the aftermath of the Chinese attacks on along the 38th parallel, Ridgway had worried that the Chinese would encircle the entire Eighth Army by exploiting the breakthrough at Chuncheon. He also lacked confidence in the UN troops' ability to hold against the Chinese offensive. On the morning of January 3, after conferring with Major General Frank W. Milburn and Major General John B. Coulter, commanders of the US I and IX Corps, respectively, Ridgway ordered the evacuation of Seoul. But with the collapse of the UN defenses at the 38th parallel, the retreat to the Seoul Bridgehead line had already started on January 1. At 0900 on January 1, Milburn ordered US I Corps to retreat to the Seoul Bridgehead line. Following his orders, the US 25th Infantry Division of the I Corps took up position at the west of Koyang, while the British 29th Independent Infantry Brigade of the I Corps had dug in at the east of Koyang. At the east of the I Corps, Coulter also ordered the withdraw of the US IX Corps at 1400 with the Anglo-Australian 27th British Commonwealth Brigade covering the rear. Some Chinese forces managed to trap the 3rd Battalion, Royal Australian Regiment (3RAR) of the 27th Commonwealth Brigade during their attacks against the ROK 6th Infantry Division, but the battalion escaped the trap with four wounded. By midnight on January 1, the US 24th Infantry Division of the IX Corps reached the Seoul Bridgehead line at the south of Uijeongbu, and the 27th Commonwealth Brigade was moved into the IX Corps rear as reserves.

But with the Chinese forces lacked the ability to siege the city, the evacuation order had caught Peng by surprise. On the morning of January 3, Peng ordered the PVA 13th Army to chase after the retreating UN forces by attack towards Seoul. The US 24th, 25th Infantry Division and the British 29th Infantry Brigade soon borne the brunt of the Chinese attacks. In US IX Corps' sector, PVA 38th Corps immediately attacked the US 24th Infantry Division as the American were trying to withdraw. In the fierce fighting that followed, the US 19th Infantry Regiment on the division's left flank was involved in numerous hand to hand struggles with the Chinese around Uijeongbu. The Chinese managed to overran the E and G company of US 19th Infantry Regiment during their attacks, but American artillery and air strikes soon inflicted 700 casualties in return. Faced with the heavy Chinese pressure, the 27th Commonwealth Brigade was again called in to cover the retreat of US IX Corps. After the US 24th Division evacuated Seoul on the night of January 3, the 27th Commonwealth Brigade started to cross the Han River on the morning of January 4, and by 0740 the entire US IX Corps had left Seoul.

On the left flank of the US 24th Infantry Division, the British 29th Infantry Brigade of the US I Corps was involved in the hardest fighting of the entire battle. In the 29th Infantry Brigade's first action of the Korean War, the brigade was ordered to defend the areas east of Koyang on the Seoul Bridgehead line. The 1st Battalion, Royal Ulster Rifles (1RUR) covered the brigade's left flank, while the 1st Battalion, Royal Northumberland Fusiliers (1RNF) was stationed on the brigade's right flank. The 1st Battalion, Gloucestershire Regiment and the Thai Battalion covered the brigade's rear with artillery support. At 0400 on January 3, 1RUR first made contact with the 149th Division of the PVA 50th Corps. The Chinese surprised and overran the B and D company of 1RUR, but a counterattack by Major C. A. H. B. Blake of 1RUR restored the battalion's position by the morning. While 1RUR was under attack, the Chinese forces also infiltrated 1RNF's positions by exploiting the unguarded valleys between hilltops occupied by the British. The entire 1RNF soon came under sniper fire and the Chinese made repeated attempts to capture the Y Company of 1RNF. To restore 1RNF's position, Brigadier Thomas Brodie of the 29th Infantry Brigade sent the W Company of 1RNF with four Churchill tanks as reinforcement. The reinforcement was met with machine gun and mortar fire, but the Chinese resistance immediately crumbled under the Churchill tanks' devastating assaults. The surviving Chinese troops fled under the bombardment from 4.2 inch mortars and 25 pounder field guns. In the aftermath of fighting, the 29th Infantry Brigade suffered at least 16 dead, 45 wounded and 3 missing, while 200 Chinese dead were found within 1RNF's position.

Soldiers from the British 29th Infantry Brigade captured by Chinese

While the British 29th Infantry Brigade and the PVA 149th Division fighting at the east of Koyang, the US 25th Infantry Division of the US I Corps started to withdraw on the left flank of 29th Infantry Brigade. The evacuation plan called for a coordinated withdraw between the US 25th Infantry Division and the British 29th Infantry Brigade in order to prevent the Chinese from infiltrating the UN rear areas, but the heavy fighting soon made the coordination between American and British units impossible. After the US 27th Infantry Regiment of the 25th Infantry Division formed the rear guard of the US I Corps, the 25th Infantry Division and the 29th Infantry Brigade were ordered to evacuate at 1500 on January 3. The 25th Infantry Division retreated with little difficulties, but the withdrawal of the 29th Infantry Brigade did not start until after dark at 2130. With the road completely open between the American rear guards and the British units, the 446th Regiment of the PVA 149th Division infiltrated UN rear areas and setup an ambush against 1RUR and the Cooper Force of the 8th King's Royal Irish Hussars. 1RUR and the Cooper Force were then quickly overran by Chinese soldiers, most of whom were completely unarmed. The Chinese had also attacked the Cromwell tanks of the Cooper Force with bundle grenades and Bangalore torpedoes, setting several on fire. In the desperate hand on hand fighting that followed, although 100 soldiers from 1RUR managed to escape the trap under the command of Major J.K.H. Shaw, Major Blake of 1RUR and Captain D. Astley-Cooper of the Cooper Force were killed in action, while another 208 British soldiers were missing in action, most of whom were captured by the Chinese. The US 27th Infantry Regiment tried to rescue the trapped British troops, but Bordie stopped the rescue in order to prevent more unnecessary losses.

With the British 29th Infantry Brigade left Seoul at 0800 on January 4, the US 27th Infantry Regiment became the last UN tactical unit that remained in the city. After fighting several more holding engagements at the outskirt of Seoul, the 27th Infantry Regiment crossed the Han River at 1400 on January 4. On January 5 Ridgway ordered the Eighth Army to withdraw from the Han River and to form a new defensive line, dubbed "Line D", at the 37th parallel between Pyeongtaek and Changhown. The Incheon port and the Gimpo (Kimpo) airfield were then demolished to deny their use to the Chinese and North Korean forces.

On the afternoon of January 4, the KPA I Corps, the PVA 38th Corps and the PVA 50th Corps entered Seoul, but they were only greeted by an empty city in flames. Most of the civilians had either fled south through the frozen Han River or evacuated to the nearby countryside. The South Korean government in Seoul, which was reduced to essential personnel before the battle, also left the city with little difficulties. A Chinese platoon reached the Seoul City Hall at about 1300 and raised the North Korean flag. On January 5, Peng ordered the PVA 50th Corps and the KPA I Corps to seize Gimpo and Incheon while instructing all other units to rest on the northern bank of the Han River. By January 7, Peng halted the Third Phase Campaign due to troop exhaustion and to prevent a repeat of the Incheon landing.

Although the UN casualties were moderate during the battle, the Third Battle of Seoul was a significant success for the Chinese military in Korea, and the UN forces' morale had sunk to its lowest point during the war. Ridgway was also extremely displeased with the performance of Eighth Army, which he had no control over due to the sudden death of Walker. Ridgway then took immediate steps to restore the morale and fighting spirit of the UN forces in Korea. With Ridgway leading the Eighth Army, MacArthur started to regain confidence in UN forces' ability to hold Korea, and the UN evacuation plan was abandoned on January 17.

Meanwhile at the UN, although the UN members and US were initially divided on how to respond to Chinese intervention in Korea, the Chinese rejection of UN ceasefire soon rallied the UN members towards US. Immediately afterward, a UN resolution that condemned China as an aggressor was passed on February 1. In the opinion of historian Bevin Alexander, the Chinese rejection of UN ceasefire had damaged the international prestige it had built from its earlier military successes, and this later made it difficult for China to either join the UN or to deny US support for Taiwan. The Korean War, which ultimately ended at the 38th parallel, would drag on for another two bloody years due to the Chinese demand for all UN forces to be withdrawn from the Korean Peninsula.

Despite its victory, the PVA had become completely exhausted after fighting nonstop since the start of the Chinese intervention. PVA Deputy Commander Han Xianchu later reported to Peng that although combat casualties had been light with only 8,500 battle casualties, the poor logistics and the exhaustion had cost the "backbone" of the Chinese forces during the Third Phase Campaign. US Far East Air Forces' "Interdiction Campaign No.4 ", which was launched on December 15, 1950 against Chinese and North Korean supply lines, also made the Chinese unable to sustain any further offensives southward. Believing that the UN forces in Korea were thoroughly demoralized and unable to counterattack, Mao finally permitted the PVA to rest for at least two to three months, while Peng and other Chinese commanders were planning for one last decisive battle in the spring of 1951. But to the surprise of Chinese commanders, Ridgway and the Eighth Army soon counterattacked the PVA with Operation Thunderbolt on January 25, 1951.

Source (edited): "http://en.wikipedia.org/wiki/Third_Battle_of_Seoul"

Battle of Hat Dich

The **Battle of Hat Dich** (3 December 1968 – 19 February 1969) was a series of military actions fought between the 1st Australian Task Force (1ATF) and the North Vietnamese Army and Viet Cong during the Vietnam War. Under the codename Operation Goodwood, two battalions from 1ATF deployed away from their base in Phuoc Tuy province, operating against suspected communist bases in the Hat Dich area, in western Phuoc Tuy, south-eastern Bien Hoa and south-western Long Khan provinces as part of a large allied sweep known as Operation Toan Thang II. The Australians conducted sustained patrolling throughout the Hat Dich and extensively ambushed tracks and river systems in the Rung Sat, occupying a series of fire support bases as operations expanded. Meanwhile American, South Vietnamese and Thai forces also operated in direct support of the Australians as part of the division-sized action.

On 6 February 1969, two additional battalions from the Thu Duc VC Regiment were reported to have entered the Hat Dich area and 4RAR/NZ was subsequently redeployed with tanks and APCs in support, resulting in the heaviest contacts of the operation. The fighting lasted 78 days and was one of the longest out of province operations mounted by the Australians during the war. Although there were few major actions, the fighting resulted in heavy Viet Cong and North Vietnamese casualties and forced them to abandon their permanent bases in the Hat Dich, as well as disrupting their preparations for an upcoming offensive during Tet. Immediately following the operation the Australians were redeployed to block the approaches towards key US and South Vietnamese bases in Bien Hoa, Long Binh and Saigon in anticipation of the 1969 Tet offensive, during Operation Federal.

Background

1968 was a turning point in the war in Vietnam. Losing more than 45,000 killed—against South Vietnamese (ARVN) and allied losses of 6,000 men—the Tet offensive had been a tactical disaster for the communists. Regardless, prior to Tet American commanders and politicians had talked confidently about winning the war, arguing that General William Westmoreland's strategy of attrition had reached the point where the communists were losing soldiers and equipment faster than they could be replaced. Yet the scale of the fighting, and the surprise and violence with which the offensive was launched, had shocked the public, contradicting such predictions of imminent victory. Confidence in the military and political leadership collapsed, as did public support for the war in America. Ultimately, Tet was a publicity and media triumph for the communists, and Hanoi emerged with a significant political victory.

The offensive had a similar effect on Australian public opinion, and caused growing uncertainty in the government about the determination of the United States to remain militarily involved in Southeast Asia. Amid the initial shock, Prime Minister John Gorton unexpectedly declared that Australia would not increase its military commitment in Vietnam beyond the current level of 8,000 personnel. The war continued without respite however, and between May and June 1968 1ATF was again deployed away from Phuoc Tuy in response to intelligence reports of another impending offensive. The Australians subsequently took up positions northeast of Saigon during Operation Toan Thang I to interdict communist lines of communication, fighting a series of significant actions over a 26-day period that became known as the Battle of Coral-Balmoral.

On 10 June 1968, General Creighton Abrams had replaced Westmoreland as commander of American and Free World Military Forces in Vietnam and the change in command had resulted in a change in both the concept of the war and its conduct. Abrams directed that the allied main effort would switch to protecting population centres, rather than searching for and attempting to destroy North Vietnamese and Viet Cong main force units as they had done previously. Equally, the prosecution of the war would increasingly be handed over to the South Vietnamese under a policy of Vietnamization, with the Americans aiming to keep North Vietnamese and Viet Cong units off balance to prevent them from interfering with resupply and reinforcement until the South Vietnamese could fight the war on their own. For the Australians the change in allied strategy foreshadowed a return to the pacification of Phuoc Tuy province. Operations outside the province over the previous eighteen months had been costly, and of the 228 Australians killed and 1,200 wounded during the war to that point almost two-thirds had been killed since January 1967.

From July, 1ATF completed a number of search-and-clear operations along the northern border areas and west of their Tactical Area of Responsibility in Phouc Tuy province. From the Nui Thi Vai and Nui Dinh hills in the west of the Phuoc Tuy, thick jungle stretched north to the junction of Bien Hoa and Long Khanh provinces, in an area known as the Hat Dich. Like the May Tao mountains in the north-east and the Long Hai hills in the south, these areas of mountains and jungle had been used extensively by the Viet Cong as base areas for many years. The Hat Dich was used by the Viet Cong because of its proximity to Saigon, as well as the important South Vietnamese and US base areas in the Long Binh–Bien Hoa complex. The Viet Cong had been using the northern border regions—including the Thua Tich and Courtenay Rubber Plantation—to link their base areas in the May Tao Mountains in the north-east with the sparsely populated but heavily vegetated Hat Dich area in the west. Over time, Australian operations in these areas usually resulted in contacts with varying size groups, including Viet Cong Main Force and occasionally North Vietnamese Army units, and ultimately led to the destruction of the communist transit and training camps, as well as a series of bunker systems and logistic storage facilities.

Prelude

By late-1968 a significant build-up of communist forces was occurring in the III Corps Tactical Zone, with 70 Main and Local Force battalions augmented by four divisions moving back from sanctuaries in Cambodia. Meanwhile the North Vietnamese had established a new unit, Headquarters Military Region 7, in order to co-ordinate operations in the area to the east and north-east of Saigon. This development, coupled with extensive communist troop movements in the Hat Dich, indicated to the South Vietnamese and their allies the possibility of an imminent offensive, possibly targeting Bien Hoa, Long Binh, Bearcat or even Saigon. Commander US II Field Force Vietnam

(IIFFV) subsequently committed 1ATF—by then commanded by Brigadier Sandy Pearson—to operations in the Hat Dich as part of a large allied sweep across Phuoc Tuy, Bien Hoa and Long Khanh provinces known as Operation Toan Thang II. The Australians would be tasked with locating and destroying Viet Cong and North Vietnamese elements in order to disrupt such an offensive and prevent Route 15 from being interdicted. To achieve this Pearson devised Operation Goodwood, planning to employ all three of his Australian battalions, supported by tanks, cavalry and artillery. Several American infantry and artillery units were also placed under his command, as were a number of South Vietnamese infantry and marine battalions. In total the allied force approached the size of a division and included nearly 10,000 men.

In early December 1968 the first Australian units were inserted into their new area of operations (AO)—known as AO Townsville—east of Saigon, halfway between Bien Hoa and Nui Dat, 30 kilometres (19 mi) to the south-east. Initially the force consisted of one infantry battalion—1st Battalion, Royal Australian Regiment (1RAR), commanded by Lieutenant Colonel Phillip Bennett—and support arms including Centurion tanks from C Squadron, 1st Armoured Regiment, M113 Armoured Personnel Carriers from A Squadron, 3rd Cavalry Regiment, 105 mm M2A2 howitzers from the batteries of 12th Field Regiment, Royal Australian Artillery and 155 mm M109 self-propelled artillery from A Battery, US 2/35 Artillery Regiment and C Battery, US 2/40 Artillery Regiment, as well as engineers from 1 Field Squadron. Later, following an extension of the AO a second battalion—at first 4RAR/NZ (ANZAC) and later 9RAR—would be deployed. It was planned to rotate the infantry battalions throughout the operation, with 1ATF intending to maintain two battalions on Operation Goodwood at all times. The concept of operations divided AO Townsville into a number of battalion sized TAORs. Headquarters 1ATF would be inserted into a fire support base (FSB), FSB Julia, situated north of the village of Thai Thein on Route QL 14 in Bien Hoa province, while 1RAR would be inserted from Nui Dat into FSB Dyke. The Australians then planned to conduct a reconnaissance-in-force, with extensive patrolling and ambushing by the infantry battalions supported by tanks and APCs, along with fire support from the field artillery batteries that would occupy a series of fire support bases as operations expanded. A number of SAS patrols were also scheduled to be inserted by air and APC to provided information on communist troop movements. The Thai Division would also operate to the north-west in AO Banglane, while 4th Battalion, 12th Infantry Regiment (detached from US 199th Light Infantry Brigade) and two troops from 3rd Battalion, 11th Armored Cavalry Regiment (3/11 ACR) as well as South Vietnamese forces from 2nd ARVN Airborne Brigade would operate in direct support of 1ATF until released.

North Vietnamese Army and Viet Cong units identified in AO Townsville included 274 VC Regiment, 74 NVA Artillery Regiment, D67 Engineer Battalion, Thu Duc Regiment, D1, D2 and D6 Sapper Reconnaissance Battalions and D440 and D445 Provincial Mobile Battalions; all under the overall command of Headquarters Military Region 7. Of particular interest to the Australians was 3 Battalion, 274 VC Regiment, which was, according to intelligence sources, believed to have recently received large numbers of North Vietnamese replacements. The battalion was estimated to include between 250 and 300 men, and was well equipped. Located in the Hat Dich, the battalion was believed to be occupying a number of permanent base camps, complete with numerous trench systems, bunkers and underground tunnels.

Battle

Initial operations in AO Townsville, 3–10 December 1968

The operation commenced on 3 December with Headquarters 1ATF moving forward by road into FSB Julia. 1RAR then deployed into FSB Dyke 6 kilometres (3.7 mi) east in the western Hat Dich, moving in APCs from A Squadron, 3rd Cavalry Regiment, along with the tanks from C Squadron, 1 Armoured Regiment and the battalion's direct support battery, 102 Field Battery. The insertion was subsequently completed successfully, with the position secured by 11:00. Initially cautious, A Company moved in AO Wondai with 2 Troop of the tank squadron, while B and C Companies followed. Yet with no immediate threat against their position detected, the Australians commenced reconnaissance-in-force operations, with D Company also moving into its assigned area, entrusting the security and defence of FSB Dyke to Support Company. Although signs of Viet Cong activity were soon located—including a freshly killed deer—there were no contacts on the first day. Meanwhile the Thais had also commenced operations in AO Banglane, and the American artillery from A Battery, US 2/35 Artillery Regiment and C Battery, US 2/40 Artillery Regiment had moved by road to occupy FSB Chestnut on the outskirts of Thai Thien in the southern sector of Bien Hoa province from where they would operate in direct support of 1ATF.

The following day, 4 December, at 08:30 C Company 1RAR encountered three small groups of Viet Cong, and a platoon attack was launched under the cover of indirect fire, with little result. Meanwhile, a bombed out bunker system was encountered by B Company from 10:00, while other minor contacts developed as the Australians continued to advance, during which they uncovered a cache of rice. At 13:47 9 Platoon C Company was briefly contacted, and during a further reconnaissance of the area the Australians located a Viet Cong camp. They subsequently withdrew, calling in an air strike with napalm to destroy the bunkers. C Company returned to the area as dusk approached and was unable to search the area until the following day. At 07:40 on 5 December the Australians assaulted the camp with the tanks, destroying a number of bunkers at point-blank range with their main armament, while the infantry grenaded the pits. Yet once again the Viet Cong were found to have fled, leaving behind one dead body from the contact the previous afternoon. The camp was estimated to be adequate for a company-sized force and was found to be untouched by the air strike the previous day, which had fallen too far west. Leaving a small force of infantry and the tanks to destroy the camp, C Company continued and was again contacted at 11:05 by three Viet Cong at close range. Pushing on however, the Australians were subsequently fired on from at least five bunkers. Bennett ordered B Company into a blocking position to the north, while the tank troop was pushed up to support C Company which was preparing to conduct a company-attack. At 15:00 the camp was assaulted and it was again found to have been abandoned. Despite locating numerous bunkers, the Australians continued to pursue the Viet Cong, however their advance was hampered by the mechanical break-down of one of the Centurions; the vehicle was subsequently recovered to FSB Dyke.

Meanwhile, the US 4/12th Battalion had come into heavy contact in AO Kilcoy and had requested assistance rather than withdrawing. Yet with 1ATF unable to provide any assets, Bennett detached two flamethrower teams from the 1RAR Assault Pioneer Platoon which were subsequently used to help extract an American platoon that had been pinned down. Between 6–10 December 1RAR continued to sweep AO Wondai, uncovering a number of ammunition caches and several freshly dug graves, however there was little contact between the Australians and the Viet Cong. To be sure, in response to the initial Australian patrols the Viet Cong had attempted to avoid contact, and had moved north away from 1ATF. Yet aggressive patrolling by 1RAR, supported by Centurion tanks and cavalry, had resulted in a number of contacts between the Australians and Viet Cong groups of up to platoon strength as they followed up the withdrawing forces. The subsequent discovery of extensive bunker systems guarded by caretaker groups, as well as the location of significant rice and weapons caches, confirmed the presence of a large communist presence in the Hat Dich, and the operation of an extensive resupply system in the area. During this time 2nd ARVN Airborne Brigade operated in AO Moose 20 kilometres (12 mi) to the north-east of FSB Julia, while US 3/11 ACR was operating to the east in AO Sherman and US 4/12th Battalion in AO Kilcoy to the west, all with minimal contact.

Expanding operations, 11–18 December 1968

The Australians were in the midst of an extensive communist resupply and staging area however, and on 11 December Pearson extended AO Townsville to take advantage of this. Under the command of Lieutenant Colonel Lee Greville, 4RAR/NZ was subsequently committed from Nui Dat in order to prevent the further northward movement of Viet Cong and North Vietnamese forces. The new battalion's area of operations—AO Kilcoy—was in Long Khan province, astride Route 15, north of Thai Thien, with its western boundary winding along the Song Thi Avi and the mangroves of the Rung Sat Special Zone. 4RAR/NZ subsequently established a fire support base with its direct support battery, 104 Field Battery, occupying FSB Sandpiper. Meanwhile, 1RAR moved to FSB Diggers Rest by helicopter, after it was secured by B Company. Patrolling continued with minor contact, a significant bunker system with interconnecting tunnels was located by the Australians late in the day. In AO Sherman US 3/11 ACR concluded operations and commenced operations to the south-west in AOs Shenandoah and Shilo, while the US 4/12th Battalion in AO Kilcoy extended its operations north-east into AO Monterey.

US forces were heavily committed in the Tay Ninh area near the Cambodian border and as a consequence 4RAR/NZ had been designated as the reserve battalion for IIFFV during the first phase of the operation, being liable to be deployed anywhere within III CTZ at short notice. Regardless, D Company deployed by APC and secured FSB Sandpiper, 1 kilometre (0.62 mi) east of Route 15, while the remainder of the battalion deployed by road. During this period 4RAR/NZ was reduced to just its three Australian rifle companies, leaving one of the New Zealand companies at the Horseshoe feature undergoing its familiarisation period, and the other at Nui Dat as the Task Force reaction force. 4RAR/NZ subsequently occupied a battalion defensive position at FSB Sandpiper, and once established the rifle companies began a patrolling and ambushing program. The requirement to be redeployed at short notice prevented the Australians from operating anymore than one hour from Sandpiper however, and this constraint also limited their effectiveness in preventing interdiction along Route 15. Regardless, continual contact was maintained throughout the operation, while the area of operations was constantly adjusted and additional fire support bases constructed as the North Vietnamese and Viet Cong attempted to bypass 1ATF, fighting to maintain the ability to resupply forces in the Hat Dich and at the same time to consolidate forces to counter the Australians. Patrolling with companies mounted in APCs, 4RAR/NZ operated west of Route 15 and conducted a number of successful ambushes. Meanwhile 1RAR continued operations in AO Wondai, the most active of the TAORs that made up AO Townsville.

On 12 December C Company 1RAR—under the command of Major Brian Honner—contacted a small Viet Cong force in a bunker system in a minor skirmish which saw the Australians capture the position after engaging with M72 rockets. Meanwhile, just after 12:00 a patrol from B Company engaged six North Vietnamese after crossing a river. Two Australians were lightly wounded in the exchange of fire. That afternoon B Company was again in contact after uncovering another bunker system and withdrew in order to destroy the complex with indirect fire. However, even as the artillery engaged the bunker system, further contacts continued with little result. By 17:00 B Company advanced once again and the lead platoon was engaged—possibly by a Viet Cong patrol leaving the bunker system previously uncovered—and the two sides exchanged fire for about 10 minutes. During this contact 12 Platoon, D Company was establishing an ambush when they were engaged by automatic weapons and RPG-2 rocket propelled grenades, which killed one Australian whose body could not be recovered until the next day. At least one Viet Cong was hit during the fighting, although further casualties could not be ascertained. The next morning B Company returned to the bunkers and found them deserted.

Later, on 13 December, C Company continued its patrol program, when at 10:00 the lead section from 7 Platoon was fired on by Viet Cong in another bunker system. Honner ordered 9 Platoon to conduct a quick attack from the right which killed two Viet Cong and captured weapons and rice. Four Australians were wounded. Further bunkers nearby were also located, although they were found to be unoccupied and were marked with a balloon for destructing by an air strike at a later date. Contacts continued throughout the afternoon with little result, while the Australians continued to uncover numerous prepared positions and bunker systems. Meanwhile, an element of US 3/11 ACR struck a booby-trap in their area of operations, losing four killed and eight wounded. At 15:00 8 Platoon had been securing a landing zone for the remainder of C Company when they heard noises to the south; a patrol subsequently clashed with five Viet Cong in a bunker system before withdrawing as artillery was called onto the position. At 17:00 7 Platoon contacted 14 Viet Cong armed with AK-47 assault rifles on the edge of a clearing, killing one while the others withdrew to a bunker system and engaged the Australians with small arms and 60 mm mortars. An assault by the Australian platoon pushed the Viet Cong out of the bunkers and they secured the area after following the withdrawing force 200 metres (220 yd) to the south-west.

At 08:40 on the morning of 14 December, 9 Platoon C Company 1RAR contacted two Viet Cong in a bunker system and killed them both. The company continued patrolling, and that afternoon at 16:05 8 Platoon contacted two more Viet Cong, killing one and uncovering a disused camp. Intelligence reports had indicated a substantial Viet Cong concentration 3 kilometres (1.9 mi) west of Tam Phuoc in Bien Hoa and in response B Company 4RAR/NZ and the 1ATF Defence and Employment Platoon moved into the area by APC. At 17:00 5 Platoon, B Company and a section of Australian cavalry contacted a party of Viet Cong, killing one and wounding another who subsequently escaped. Further Viet Cong were observed moving west out of the battalion's AO, with elements of US 3/17 Air Cavalry Regiment subsequently deployed. The following day C Company 1RAR continued searching and ambushing in AO Wondai after detecting the presence of parties of Viet Cong who had likely been caught by surprise by the Australian patrols. Around 10:30 four Viet Cong approached 8 Platoon and were engaged with small arms; returning fire with RPGs which slightly wounded three Australians, three Viet Cong were then killed while a sweep by the Australians failed to locate the fourth. That afternoon D Company also uncovered an unoccupied bunker system, while A and B Company each had minor contacts, with 4 Platoon killing one Viet Cong around 16:00. Later, at 17:20 6 Platoon B Company was contacted by five Viet Cong at 30 metres (33 yd) while deploying into an ambush site, badly wounding the platoon commander; two Viet Cong were also hit. The Viet Cong then withdrew while the platoon sergeant took over command of the Australian platoon, and during the subsequent sweep one body was found. Meanwhile in AO Kilcoy 9 Platoon C Company 4RAR/NZ located three Viet Cong in a camp. A section then assaulted the camp opening fire at 15 metres (16 yd), killing one Viet Cong and wounding the other two who escaped; a PPSh sub-machine gun, an SKS assault rifle and an M1 carbine were subsequently captured.

Although the had been no major actions during the first half of December, there had been 40 contacts in the 1ATF area of operations, resulting in 22 Viet Cong killed, two wounded and two more possible killed, as well as 20 weapons captured, 66 mines, 153 grenades, 17 mortar rounds, 26 RPG-2 rockets, 50 kilograms (110 lb) of explosive and 26,380 small arms rounds. Most of the communist dead were Viet Cong Main Force soldiers, while some were North Vietnamese, however no unit had been identified. Meanwhile, the Thais had also reported eight contacts in the Binh Son rubber plantation. On 16 December the platoons from 1RAR continued patrolling and ambushing, and over the following two days the Australians and Viet Cong fought a number of fleeting contacts resulting in at least two Viet Cong being killed. In AO Kilcoy 4RAR/NZ also continued patrolling, with a sentry from 5 Platoon B Company killing one Viet Cong which had followed the platoon after it had halted for their midday meal. Later on the evening of 17 December 1ATF intelligence had reported the possible presence of a large Viet Cong force of 500 men in the Phuoc Hoa forest, while an unidentified artillery unit was believed to be preparing to attack Long Thanh and Binh Son with mortars after leaving the Thai AO.

However, that night there was little activity in the Australian AO, while at 03:15 on 18 December an ARVN outpost was attacked, resulting in two Viet Cong killed and three South Vietnamese wounded before a US reaction force arrived from Bearcat. The following day both 1RAR and 4RAR/NZ continued operations with minor contact; a camp of four small bunkers was located by 1 Platoon A Company 1RAR, while at 09:20 3 Platoon discovered the bodies of two men that had likely also been killed during the contact with 2 Platoon on the 16th. Later that day 1 Platoon found another 11 bunkers located on the southern bank of the Suoi Cau Moi and they were destroyed the following day. Meanwhile, 12 Platoon D Company 4RAR/NZ contacted two Viet Cong at 16:21, killing one and capturing an AK-47. Around 19:00 that evening a helicopter operating in direct support of 1RAR observed red and white flashlights in the Australian AO and they were engaged by 102 Field Battery.

Fighting in late-December 1968

The next morning, 19 December, an Australian patrol from the 1RAR Anti-Tank Platoon searched the engagement area and reported finding nothing of significance. The Australian platoons continued to patrol however, and at 08:49 9 Platoon C Company engaged a group of six Viet Cong at 50 metres (55 yd) while crossing a creek, killing two and wounding a third. Just after midday 2 Platoon A Company had been moving in column parallel to a track when they were ambushed by a Viet Cong force in an undetected bunker system. Both the front and rear Australian sections were engaged with small arms, while the centre section was targeted by two claymore mines; heavy casualties resulted with the Australians losing one killed and 10 wounded. In response the remainder of A Company moved quickly to support the beleaguered platoon, while artillery fired on the bunkers. The evacuation of the casualties was complete by 15:20, following which the Australians assaulted the camp, only to find that the Viet Cong had withdrawn. With the light beginning to fail, 8 Platoon C Company heard noises in the scrub and observed a group of 10 Viet Cong in a nearby camp. At 17:45 the Australians moved in, killing one and forcing the remainder to withdraw.

Meanwhile in AO Kilcoy 4RAR/NZ continued to experience only minor contact. 10 Platoon D Company had been deployed in a blocking position at a track junction on 19 December and had contacted a group of five Viet Cong at 13:38 after they had approached the Australian position. The sentry opened fire with his M60 machine-gun at 40 metres (44 yd) killing one and probably wounding two more. The surviving Viet Cong went to ground and returned fire, wounding two Australians before successfully withdrawing. 2 SAS Squadron also continued reconnaissance patrols in AO Sternum, killing one Viet Cong during a clash at 10:30. The same day in AO Moose, B and D Companies from the South Vietnamese 11th Airborne Battalion had also contacted a large Viet Cong force at 13:00, estimated to include at least two platoons armed with AK-47s and RPK light machine-guns. The fighting continued until last light and resulted in heavy ARVN casualties which included six killed and six wounded. Communist casualties were unknown.

On the morning of 20 December A Company 1RAR found a Viet Cong surgical facility and dispensary, and capturing a quantity of rice, salt and documents. At 09:20 9 Platoon C Company ambushed seven Viet Cong moving south on a track, killing three of them and capturing an AK-47. Only one of the Viet Cong had been armed, while the other two had been carrying packs filled with food and tobacco. Ten minutes later 8 Platoon ambushed two Viet Cong moving along a track away from 9 Platoon, killing one and also capturing an AK-47. Moving on, the Australian platoon was in contact again at 10:50, with the lead sections killing a Viet Cong soldier in a bunker and uncovering a cache. Later A Company uncovered another large, unoccupied bunker complex and quantities of food, medical supplies, explosives and ammunition. As with the previous bunker systems the Australians proceeded to destroy them with explosives, with A Company 1RAR destroying 93 bunkers over the previous three days. On dusk 1 Platoon was establishing its night ambush location when it had a fleeting contact at 17:55. The same day in the 4RAR/NZ AO, a composite platoon protecting a survey party contacted a group of five Viet Cong without result, while W Company on the Horseshoe feature had a successful ambush, killing two Viet Cong and wounding a third.

At 03:00 on 21 December, FSB Redhat 3 in AO Moose—occupied by elements of 2nd ARVN Airborne Brigade—came under sustained mortar fire and ground attack by up to two Viet Cong companies. The mortaring ceased at 04:00 and the attack was finally repelled by 05:40, with the South Vietnamese following up as the Viet Cong attempted to withdraw to south and south-east. 5 Airborne Battalion maintained contact with the withdrawing forces, while 11 Airborne Battalion moved north-east into a blocking position. Supported by artillery and helicopter gunships the South Vietnamese inflicted heavy casualties on their attackers before the fighting finally ceased at 06:15. South Vietnamese losses included two killed and 12 wounded, and one American advisor wounded. Viet Cong casualties were 29 killed and two wounded, while a large quantity of weapons were also recovered by the South Vietnamese. The attacking force was later identified as two companies from 274 VC Regiment. Meanwhile in the AO Wondai, it was planned that B, C and D Companies 1RAR would continue to ambush on 21 December, while A Company would cross the Suoi Cau Moi to establish blocking positions around the Binh Son rubber plantation. At 10:30 A Company discovered a cache of medical supplies before cautiously crossing the creek. On the northern bank they uncovered 15 recently used bunkers and the graves of five Viet Cong, four of which were believed to have also been killed in a contact with 8 Platoon C Company on 13 December. While moving into a new ambush position, 6 Platoon B Company also discovered an extensive bunker system and the company remained in place to destroy it the following day. Meanwhile A Company also reported destroying a further 30 bunkers.

The following day, 22 December, 1RAR continued ambushing and patrolling, with A and B Companies continuing to destroy the bunkers located the previous day, while C and D Companies maintained their ambush positions. A small bunker system was located during the day but there was no further contact. Meanwhile at 18:00 the

Australians received reports of heavy fighting outside of their area of operations, with a company from the 1/43 ARVN Regiment coming under heavy mortar fire, before being assaulted by a reinforced Viet Cong battalion from 274 VC Regiment. The South Vietnamese were supported by AC-47 Spooky gunships, helicopter light fire teams, fast air and US and Thai artillery and were reinforced by elements of the 1/48 ARVN Regiment. Meanwhile at 22:00 a Viet Cong company was observed moving from the south to reinforce the battle which continued until 00:30 when the communists finally broke contact. Meanwhile other South Vietnamese units had also been attacked during the evening, with the fighting resulting in a total 50 Viet Cong killed, while South Vietnamese losses included 13 killed and 50 wounded. Also that evening, elements of 2 Troop, A Squadron, 3rd Cavalry Regiment had been occupying an ambush site on a track 2.5 kilometres (1.6 mi) west of Route 15, northeast of Phu My in Phuoc Tuy province. At 23:58 the ambush was sprung, killing six Viet Cong and capturing another, while 13 oxcarts were also destroyed.

The next day at 12:00 on 23 December in AO Kilcoy, 8 Platoon, C Company 4RAR/NZ mounted in APCs had been reacted to a reported sighting of Viet Cong. The platoon was split into two, with one half under the platoon sergeant moving forward on foot to search the area, moving through open rice padi parallel with the dense scrub. When the patrol came level with a break in the vegetation it was suddenly engaged with a claymore-type command detonated mine, wounding five members of the platoon. In response the remaining half of the platoon swept the area forward of the engagement area, however the Viet Cong made good their escape, withdrawing by sampan down a branch of a nearby river. One of the wounded Australians subsequently died of his wounds before the evacuation of the casualties could be arranged. Meanwhile the Christmas cease-fire began at 18:00, but was broken after the Viet Cong attacked elements of 2nd ARVN Airborne Brigade at FSB Barbara with mortars and small arms fire. Australian and South Vietnamese artillery and helicopter light fire teams were subsequently called-in to provide support.

On Christmas Day a special dinner was prepared by the 4RAR/NZ cooks and trucked to the battalion at FSB Sandpiper in AO Kilcoy. Likewise with 1RAR still deployed in AO Wondai, a Christmas lunch was prepared and flown to the rifle companies, while the Australians at FSB Julia also enjoyed a traditional Christmas Day lunch, with the other ranks served by the officers and sergeants. Although the allied units continued to observe the cease-fire there were a number of minor violations initiated by Viet Cong and North Vietnamese units. Soon after lunch an RPG round destroyed an American jeep on Route 15, and a number of Australian tanks and APCs, along with the Task Force Headquarters Defence and Employment Platoon were reacted. The Australians engaged the area with machine-gun fire and the infantry swept the area, uncovering numerous tracks but little else. Later, in AO Wondai 10 Platoon 1RAR was fired on by two Viet Cong at 14:07, and they subsequently captured an AK-47. Meanwhile over the evening of 25/26 December South Vietnamese forces at FSB Barbara in AO Moose came under small arms and mortar fire, suffering a number of wounded. In AO Wondai on 26 December A, B, and C Companies 1RAR were to redeploy to new ambush locations, while D Company moved north to ambush Route 320 following a further extension of the area of operations. At 09:55, while moving to a new position 8 Platoon, C Company contacted seven Viet Cong carrying packs filled with food, clothes and detonators, killing two and capturing an AK-47.

On 27 December, after being released as III CTZ reserve, 4RAR/NZ was deployed further north to the border between Long Khanh and Bien Hoa province. Flying-in to AO Warragul in order to more effectively prevent communist interdiction of Route 15, the battalion established FSB Wattle, a position which had been used by the Australians previously during Operation Hawkesbury in September. This move proved unsuccessful however, with the North Vietnamese and Viet Cong nowhere to be found. That morning in AO Wondai, 1 Platoon A Company 1RAR was watching the northern bank of Suoi Cau Moi and at 07:45 they contacted three Viet Cong as they attempted to cross the creek, killing one. Thirty minutes later 7 Platoon, C Company had been engaged by two Viet Cong while moving into a new ambush location. In response the Australians swept the area, and were subsequently contacted by 10 to 15 Viet Cong in a bunker system with small arms, RPG-2s and a claymore mine, resulting in one killed and five wounded, including the platoon commander, Lieutenant Bob Convery. More than 1,000 metres (1,100 yd) away, Honner moved quickly to bring the remainder of C Company to the aid of the platoon in contact. Meanwhile 7 Platoon had pulled back from the bunkers moving their casualties to a position where they could be winched up through the canopy for Dustoff. The casualty evacuation was complete by 11:00, while Convery had continued to co-ordinate fire support for his platoon despite his wounds. By the time C Company arrived the battle was over, however following preparation by artillery the Australians assaulted the camp, only to find that the Viet Cong had withdrawn; it was destroyed the next day. That afternoon Australian cavalry from 1 Troop occupied an ambush site 2 kilometres (1.2 mi) south-west of FSB Julia, near one of the tributaries of the Rung Sat. At 17:20 the ambush was sprung, killing one Viet Cong and capturing a quantity of rice after sinking a sampan.

Between 28–30 December only minor contact occurred in AO Warragul, with C Company 4RAR/NZ fing six separate bunker systems—many of which were fully developed with overhead protection and communication trenches—confirming the intelligence view that the area was likely the base and training are for a number Viet Cong main force units. Elsewhere, after handing over the defences on the Horseshoe to V Company, W Company flew north on 31 December to join the battalion. Meanwhile 1RAR continued operations in AO Wondai with minor contact.

Action continues, 1–20 January 1969

On 1 January 1969 Pearson moved 9RAR from Nui Dat to relieve 1RAR in the Long Thanh district of Bien Hoa province. Under the command of Lieutenant Colonel Alan Morrison, the battalion subsequently took over operations in AO Wondai. Supported by 161 Battery RNZA they occupied FSB Diggers Rest. The battalion then mounted a series of company sweeps through the area while watching for large-scale movement of North Vietnamese and Viet Cong forces. For the Australians, Operation Goodwood then became a 'cat and mouse' game, with 1ATF manoeuvring in the hope of engaging the Viet Cong in order to destroy their bases and restricting their movement. Meanwhile the North Vietnamese and Viet Cong struggled to maintain their resupply system, and in response to this pressure they opted to disperse in an attempt to bypass the Australians, only consolidating to fight when an opportunity to arose to inflict a setback on the allies. Meanwhile, a number of SAS patrols were inserted by air and road on 6 January 1969 to gather information on communist troop movements. Further patrols were deployed to the southern Bien Hoa-Firestone Trail area in mid-January, while additional SAS patrols were inserted on 29 January in an attempt to ascertain communist troop movements.

On 2 January 1RAR was immediately redeployed on Operation Tiger Balm to conduct a cordon-and-search of Xom My Xuan and Lang Phuoc Hoa, along Highway 15. This operation was designed to support Goodwood, as it was believed that the Viet Cong infrastructure had moved into the villages along the highway after being forced out of the jungle during 1ATFs operations there. The search was completed by 12:00 on 4 January and the operation concluded have only achieved modest results for the Australians. During this period South Vietnamese forces had continued to operate in AO Moose with minimal contact. Yet at 16:40 on 7 January B Company, 5 Airborne Battalion was contacted by a Viet Cong squad resulting in five South Vietnamese being wounded, two of whom later died of their wounds. The Viet Cong had then withdrawn and their casualties could not be determined. Meanwhile 4RAR/NZ began a sweep in their allocated area just inside the Phuoc Tuy border in AO Warrigul, settling into a routine of movement by day and harbouring at night while covered by the guns of 104 Battery at FSB Wattle. Ambushing on tracks continued to prove successful. On 1 January 4 Platoon B Company ambushed a track, killing one Viet Cong, while later 7 Platoon C Company found a cache of twenty 82 mm mortar rounds, twenty 57 mm recoilless rifle rounds and 40 grenades. On 3 January 9 Platoon C Company was forced to spring an ambush during set up, killing two Viet Cong soldiers and capturing their packs. Because of the frequency that the Viet Cong were continuing to use the tracks in the AO the ambush remained in location. Less than an hour later, while in a company defensive position, the 6 Platoon B Company sentry contacted three Viet Cong soldiers moving outside the perimeter, killing one before withdrawing back the defensive position under the covering fire of the section machine-gun. The two surviving Viet Cong then fled back along the track away from 6 Platoon, only to be killed by 5 Platoon who was also ambushing the track.

Throughout January patrols from 9RAR had fought small groups of Viet Cong daily, and on occasions encountered groups of platoon and sometimes company-sized. Numerous bunker complexes and camps were also uncovered. Although most contacts were minor, at times these encounters led to prolonged fighting. At 12:20 on 5 January 4 Platoon, B Company contacted five Viet Cong and in the ensuing action two were killed while one Australian died of wounds. At the same time D Company contacted a Viet Cong base camp, losing five men wounded. The following day 5 Platoon, B Company was contacted at 12:00 and suffered one killed and five wounded, while the Assault Pioneer Platoon later uncovered a sizeable cache of ammunition. On 10 January, A Company struck a large bunker system and was engaged with heavy machine-guns which pinned down an Australian platoon. During the company action that ensued the remaining to Australian platoons conducted a flanking assault with bayonets fixed under the cover of mortars and artillery. Two Australians were killed and the battle continued for three-and-a-half hours until last light. Another assault the following morning by A Company supported by tanks found the camp abandoned by the Viet Cong. Meanwhile in AO Warrigul 4RAR/NZ continued to find a number of small camps and bunker systems. During the morning D Company had had a number of fleeting contacts while setting up ambush locations and had also located a battalion-sized bunker system. However at 16:30 11 Platoon D Company contacted up to 10 Viet Cong in a bunker system, and in the ensuing clash the Australians killed two before withdrawing under the cover of artillery due to the weight of defensive fire. An air strike was subsequently used to destroy the camp, probably killing three more Viet Cong. A sweep of the area by the Australians at first light the next day found no weapons or any other material. Late on the evening of 11 January a New Zealand soldier from 3 Platoon, W Company was accidentally killed by friendly fire after firing broke out in response to noises heard on the company perimeter; an incident which clearly illustrated the difficulties and dangers of operating in the jungle at night. Two days 4RAR/NZ was relieved by 1RAR, and returned to Nui Dat.

In AO Wondai on 13 January 8 Platoon C Company 9RAR contacted two Viet Cong at 09:15, killing one and capturing an AK-47 and a pack. Soon after B Company discovered an unoccupied camp and captured a quantity of equipment including a 60 mm mortar and base plate, rifles and ammunition. Several hours later A Company located a disused camp and a bunker system, uncovering grenades and explosives. Eight bodies were also discovered, and they were believed to have been killed during the contact three days before. Meanwhile, even with 1RAR nearing the end of its tour of duty it was committed to Operation Goodwood once more, and was tasked with ambushing communist lines of communication and conducting reconnaissance-in-force operations if required. On 13 January Bennett moved to establish FSB Margaret 1 kilometre (0.62 mi) east of Tam Phuoc in Bien Hoa province, located in AO Kilcoy immediately west of AO Wondai. That morning at 07:30 C Company commenced the fly-in, securing the fire support base while Support Company and 102 Field Battery departed Nui Dat by road. B Company subsequently flew-in to FSB Chestnut to secure the area for the road convoy until it was called forward to FSB Margaret, and was followed by A and D Companies which were air-lifted by helicopter. The Australians then commenced an operation to search part of the Rung Sat, locating a number of small camps among the mangroves and swamps. At last light 6 Platoon B Company 1RAR contacted three Viet Cong, and the next morning one body and an AK-47 were discovered. Meanwhile in AO Moose, the 2nd ARVN Brigade had concluded operations on 15 January and was relieved in place by A Brigade of the ARVN Marine Regiment, with the 1st Marine Battalion occupying FSB Kathleen and 5th Marine Battalion occupying FSB Barbara.

Later, in AO Wondai on the afternoon of 16 January, 40 Viet Cong were sighted in a camp and were engaged with artillery. C Company 9RAR, under the command of Major Laurie Lewis, was rapidly redeployed by helicopter just prior to last light. The company moved on foot to its objective, and set up a night ambush. At 23:20 the ambush was initiated by 8 Platoon, when approximately 15 North Vietnamese soldiers carrying torches entered the engagement area; five were killed in the action. At first light C Company entered and searched the now abandoned camp, 300 metres (330 yd) from the ambush site, and aside from a number of dead killed previously by artillery nothing of note was discovered. In contrast, 1RAR had continued to operate with only minor contact in AO Kilcoy, ambushing a number of waterways. However on the evening of 16 January at 20:50 9 Platoon C Company fired on a sampan, engaging the vessel at 50 metres (55 yd) with an M60 machine-gun, small arms and grenades, killing two Viet Cong. The Australians then used flares to illuminate any swimmers but nothing further was observed. Later at 11:43 on 18 January in AO Kilcoy a section of Australian APCs from A Squadron Headquarters was deployed to resupply D Company 1RAR when an APC hit a large road-mine 8 kilometres (5.0 mi) west of Thai Thien on Route 15, killing the crew commander and wounding two others, and destroying the vehicle. Later as Goodwood continued the Viet Cong mined roads and tracks extensively, hampering the operations of the Australian cavalry and causing further damage to vehicles and injuries to personnel. At dusk an ambush from 6 Platoon B Company had engaged two Viet Cong, and although one soldier was seen to fall no casualties were found during the sweep. At 06:15 the following morning an ambush by 4 Platoon B Company contacted a group of five Viet Cong, killing one and wounding a second. Around 07:00 B Company 1RAR observed a large force of 70 Viet Cong moving from north-west to south-east, wearing greens and carrying large packs. They were subsequently engaged by artillery, while A Company moved into blocking positions by APC to the south-west and B Company commenced a sweep to the east. Much of the artillery fire had been inaccurate however, and the sweeps were completed without incident. At 12:00 D Company was inserted by air to the west, and also swept the area without incident.

In a series of incidents on the morning of 19 January, all four of 9RARs rifle companies, as well as the battalion's Support Company, were in contact at the same time during heavy fighting. So frenetic was the action that 161 Battery RNZA were only just able to change their supporting fires from one target to another, while the 9RAR Mortar Platoon was also used to hit multiple dispersed targets with their indirect fires. Three Australians were subsequently killed and five wounded, all from 2 Platoon A Company, after rocket propelled grenades were fired into the company position. The same day an Australian soldier was accidentally killed during a patrol by the 9RAR Anti-Tank Platoon. On 20 January, another Australian was killed during an action against a Viet Cong bunker. These actions were having some effect however, and reports suggested that a communist regiment was attempting to move north through AO Wondai, but were being delayed by successful patrolling by 9RAR. Consequently 9RAR continued its blocking operation. Intelligence received in mid-January highlighted the success of these operations, with 274 VC Regiment believed to be encountering serious morale problems, due in part, to a lack of food.

Meanwhile, after watching a well used track for a number of days 2 Troop, A Squadron, 3rd Cavalry Regiment together with an SAS patrol, established an ambush 5 kilometres (3.1 mi) east of FSB Chestnut in Bien Hoa province on 19 January. At 17:16 the ambush was sprung against a large communist force, resulting in three killed and two wounded. The survivors were able to successfully withdraw however, and they waited until after dark to counter-attack the Australians. The SAS were subsequently forced to withdraw as the APCs provided covering fire while another three Viet Cong were probably killed in the fighting. The same evening 3 Troop mounted a successful ambush close to FSB Chestnut, killing one Viet Cong and wounding another three. These ambushes were two of a number conducted by the Australian cavalry throughout the operation, and they utilised a new, more aggressive technique with considerable success. Indeed during this period 10 successful ambushes were mounted in the Hat Dich area using the new tactics devised by the squadron's Intelligence Officer after working with the US Army during previous operations. Three weeks later three graves were discovered 1 kilometre (0.62 mi) west of FSB Chestnut and it was believed that they had also been killed during the 2 Troop ambush mounted on 19 January. Later, on 20 January 1 Troop was deployed on a reconnaissance-in-force operation approximately 5 kilometres (3.1 mi) south of FSB Julia in Bien Hoa province. At 09:44 one of the APCs detonated a anti-tank mine, wounding five Australians. The same day the South Vietnamese A Marine Brigade and 1st Marine Battalion departed AO Moose. HQ 52 ARVN Regiment relieved them, augmented by 3/52 ARVN Regiment and the 5th Marine Battalion which remained attached in direct support. Operations continued with little contact however.

Operations in late-January 1969
1RAR redeployed on 21 January, with A Company moving west back to Route 15 to ambush the area and C Company moving back into AO Wondai by APC to sweep a key ridgeline. Meanwhile B and D Companies continued to search and ambush in AO Kilcoy, while Thai units completed a reconnaissance-in-force south from the Binh Son area. That afternoon A Company relieved D Company, which continued on towards FSB Julia to establish ambush positions in the vicinity of Thai Thien. Meanwhile C Company had completed its sweep without incident. That evening 12 Viet Cong moving from east to west entered the killing ground of an ambush mounted by 10 Platoon D Company. The ambush was sprung at 21:10 with claymore mines and small arms at a range of less the 2 metres (6.6 ft), hitting two of them. A sweep at first light the following morning found one dead, an AK-47 and marks where another wounded soldier had been dragged towards the village. At 09:15 the following day D Company searched an area where air strikes had revealed what were believed to be tunnels and a camp, and they uncovered a number of bunker systems. 12 Platoon subsequently engaged two Viet Cong, wounding one and capturing him; he was administered morphine before he died of his wounds. A subsequent search of the area uncovered another bunker system. Meanwhile that afternoon C Company had completed its search without incident and returned to AO Kilcoy. That evening 11 Platoon D Company was contacted at 19:15 while moving into a night ambush, killing one Viet Cong soldier.

A Company 1RAR completed its redeployment by APC at 10:10 on 23 January, while C Company moved to FSB Margaret. That evening at 20:50 10 Platoon D Company ambushed a group of Viet Cong, killing two. On 24 January C Company 1RAR conducted a reconnaissance-in-force against a suspected communist logistic transfer point, while a combat engineer team was detached to the battalion, along with a troop of APCs and a troop of tanks. That morning at 09:25 a number of bunkers were located by 8 Platoon, while forty-four 50-kilogram (110 lb) bags of rice and two bags of salt were found by the Assault Pioneer Platoon. A Company had found three fresh graves during the day, which were believed to have been killed during recent SAS operations in the area, while a number of small camps and a quantity of weapons, clothing and rice were also uncovered. Meanwhile B Company was redeployed to block Viet Cong movement through Phu My. That afternoon a patrol from 7 Platoon B Company had clashed with ten to fifteen Viet Cong at 17:41, killing one at close range. At the same time 3 Platoon A Company was also in contact, wounding one Viet Cong soldier. Later at 18:57 11 Platoon D Company fired on two Viet Cong who returned fire, wounding one Australian. B Company operations east of Phu My continued on 25 January, with an ambush by 6 Platoon firing on a number of oxcarts at 05:45; later it was discovered that a local villager had been wounded after ignoring the curfew. Meanwhile 1RAR continued operations over the coming days with only minor contact which resulted in several Viet Cong being wounded and a number of rice caches located by the Australians before they moved to secure pick-up zones on the afternoon of 26 January in order to prepare for extraction the following day.

On 27 January 4RAR/NZ redeployed to the Hat Dich to replace 1RAR which had returned to Nui Dat that day, following a few weeks respite during which W Company 4RAR/NZ had carried out a three-day operation with an ARVN unit in the Long Green. B Company moved by APC to the old FSB Dyke position and secured it for the fly-in of Battalion Headquarters and D Company. W Company rejoined the battalion the following day, deploying by APC east of Phuoc Tuy border in response to information from SAS patrols of significant Viet Cong movement in this area. Operating in AO Riversdale to the west of FSB Julia in an area close to that which they had in mid-December—now extended further east—the rifle companies then swept an area of jungle 10 kilometres (6.2 mi) north-east of Thai Thien on Route 15. On 29 January W Company clashed heavy with a company-sized communist force. During stand-to that evening the New Zealanders had heard the sounds of movement through the bamboo and a short but fierce engagement ensued with W Company being hit by heavy machine-gun fire and rocket propelled grenades from three directions, wounding three men. W Company successfully resisted the assault however, firing their M60 machine-guns and more than 15 claymore mines, while artillery fire was called-in to break up the attack. Blood trials and drag marks found the following morning indicated that as many as five Viet Cong had been killed. SAS patrols had been operating in the area prior to the arrival of W Company and it is probable that previous contacts during the day had led the Viet Cong to believe that they had located a five man reconnaissance patrol rather than a New Zealand rifle company. The same day

9RARs AO was extended westward, with FSB Jenny established to cover the operations of B, C and D Company south of Route 15 following indications of an imminent attack against Long Thanh. Meanwhile A Company returned to Nui Dat to refit. The expected attack never eventuated however, and these operations proved uneventful, with the battalion redeploying to its original AO two days later.

4RAR/NZ had begun to meet strong resistance within its AO. On 30 January all four rifle companies clashed with small two to five-man groups of Viet Cong with in the space of a few hours, killing five and uncovering another camp as well as quantities of ammunition, medical supplies and rice. Meanwhile after an uneventful period at the Horseshoe, V Company joined 4RAR/NZ following its relief-in-place by C Company. After landing V Company commenced moving towards it patrol area and soon found itself in an entrenched camp, locating a number of caches. An ambush was then established on tracks approaching the bunker system by 3 Platoon, who killed three Viet Cong over the following two days. The next day, 31 January D Company contacted one Viet Cong soldier at 09:15 without result and the Australians subsequently attempted to follow-up. An hour later 10 Platoon was ambushed with claymore mines, rocket propelled grenades and small arms by five to 10 Viet Cong soldiers located in a bunker system, killing two Australians and wounding two more. The Australians resisted strongly however, and the platoon's fire eventually forced the Viet Cong to break contact and withdraw west. During the opening burst of fire Private Malcolm Gibson, an acting section commander, had been knocked unconscious and after recovering he crawled forward under heavy fire to man the machine-gun, providing covering fire to his section despite having the pack shot off his back. He then regrouped his men and provided effective fire support for the remainder the platoon. For his leadership and courage he was later awarded the Distinguished Conduct Medal.

Renewed fighting, 1–16 February 1969

On 1 February in AO Moose the South Vietnamese 5th Marine Battalion suffered two killed and six wounded following the detonation of an anti-personnel mine. Later that evening Australian cavalry from 3 Troop ambushed the edge of the waterway to the southwest of FSB Julia in Bien Hoa province. The ambush was sprung at 02:08, and resulted in two Viet Cong killed and one sampan sunk. Meanwhile during the mid-afternoon in AO Riverdale, 3 Platoon V Company contacted a number of Viet Cong, killing one and capturing an M16 assault rifle, while after last light 5 Platoon B Company sprung a night ambush, killing one and wounding another and capturing an AK47, an SKS and a number of M16 magazine. That afternoon 11 Platoon D Company 4RAR/NZ had also found a camp and eight graves; however there was no further contact between the Australians and Viet Cong in AO Riverdale for the next five days, although on 4 February W Company 4RAR/NZ found an Viet Cong camp containing 60 bunkers which was subsequently searched and then destroyed. Meanwhile in AO Wondai B Company 9RAR subsequently conducted a number of successful ambushes and on 4 February 5 Platoon ambushed a Viet Cong party of eight men at first light, killing six of them.

In AO Riverdale on 6 January, B Company 4RAR/NZ had patrolled into the D Company AO, and soon after 4 Platoon contacted two Viet Cong, killing both and capturing two AK-47s and two packs. Soon after 5 Platoon uncovered five fresh graves which were likely the result of a previous action. Meanwhile two additional battalions from the Thu Duc VC Regiment were reported to have entered the Hat Dich area. Pearson subsequently redeployed 4RAR/NZ the following day, and with tanks and APCs in support the battalion moved by helicopter into AO Tiki to the north-west along Route 15, where it would become engaged in the heaviest contacts of Operation Goodwood. Greville subsequently establish FSB Janice in the rice fields at the northern end of the Rung Sat mangrove swamps. A number of successful ambushes were conducted by the Australian infantry over the coming days, while patrolling by day resulted in the discovery of a number of large weapons caches. Indeed, although tactically questionable, the Viet Cong had continued to use many of the same routes and tracks throughout the operation despite suffering heavy casualties during these ambushes. Meanwhile, overnight Australian cavalry from 3 Troop had been deployed in a night ambush 3 kilometres (1.9 mi) west of Phu My, adjacent to Route 15 on the edge of the Rung Sat. A motorised junk and a sampan were subsequently sunk and three Viet Cong killed by the Australians.

On 8 February, D Company 9RAR was contacted in the north-east of their AO with RPGs and small arms by a platoon-size force in a bunker system. Heavy fighting ensured with the action lasting five hours as the Australians called in mortar and artillery fire, and were also supported by air strikes and helicopter light fire teams. The lead Australian platoon—12 Platoon—had suffered one wounded during the initial contact, and a further five were wounded as the sweep continued. Due to the heavy fire the evacuation of the wounded was delayed, and the Dustoff helicopter was forced to depart without the casualties, one of whom subsequently died of his wounds. A number of Viet Cong snipers in trees had also engaged the Australians, in conjunction with the troops in the bunkers and the area was subsequently bombarded by the Australians with artillery, helicopter light fire teams and air strikes before 12 Platoon was able to break contact. Five Viet Cong were believed to have been killed. Later during the subsequent follow-up over the next two days, the Australian found an extensive complex of four bunker systems with a total of over 60 mutually supporting bunkers. Meanwhile at last light in AO Tiki, 3 Platoon V Company 4RAR/NZ observed around 35 Viet Cong moving west out of the area of operations and they were engaged by artillery and helicopter light fire teams. The Viet Cong responded with small arms, firing on the helicopters before withdrawing under the cover of darkness after suffering a number of casualties. The following day the New Zealanders conducted a sweep of the area and recovered one body. Meanwhile 52 ARVN Regiment concluded operations in AO Moose and commenced operations in AO Warragul.

The following day, 9 February, contacts continued between the New Zealanders and the Viet Cong. At 14:38 a section patrol from 2 Platoon W Company 4RAR/NZ clashing with five Viet Cong at 10 metres (33 ft) while conducting a reconnaissance of a track, killing two and capturing an AK-47 and a pistol. A follow-up sweep by 2 Platoon located a small camp and five packs. Further fleeting contacts occurred during the afternoon and early evening, before V Company sighted 10 Viet Cong at 19:50 from their night position and subsequently engaged them with artillery. At first light the next morning the New Zealanders were contacted while checking the area of the previous night's engagement and one Viet Cong was killed. That evening V Company again observed 14 Viet Cong moving through their area of operations and they again directed artillery onto them. The Viet Cong subsequently withdrew carrying two bodies, while a sweep early the next morning resulted in the New Zealanders capturing a pack containing four pistols and three AK-47 magazines. Later four dead Viet Cong were found and were believed to have been the result of the previous contact with V Company on the 10th, while B Company nearby also found a dead body in the area engaged by the New Zealanders.

Later, during a search in AO Wondai on the afternoon of 14 February, C Company 9RAR contacted a strong Viet Cong force in a large bunker system. Despite being supported by a helicopter light fire team and artillery the Australians were unable to advance, and they subsequently broke contact in order to allow the use of medium artillery after having lost one killed and four wounded. The following day A Company was deployed with tanks to assist a further assault by C Company in the bunker system, which was again found to have been abandoned by the Viet Cong after having suffered a number of casualties. Meanwhile a series of minor contacts occurred as communist forces began returning to the area. In AO Tiki, D Company 4RAR/NZ mounted a series of ambushes on the creeks which flowed into the Rung Sat. The Viet Cong had been using these watercourses extensively for logistic resupply and to gain access to the villages in the area. On 15 February 10 Platoon D Company had deployed to southern end of the battalion AO in order to mount a night ambush on a high bank on a sharp bend in the Suoi Cau river. The infantry were reinforced by 90 mm M67 recoilless rifles (RCLs) from the Tracker Platoon, which were placed on the flanks. At 21:03 six sampans carrying around 15 Viet Cong entered the engagement area moving from west to east and the ambush was initiated by splintex rounds from the RCLs as well as M60 machine-guns and small arms. At least two sampans were sunk and six Viet Cong killed before they were able to withdraw to the southern bank and engage the Australians with small arms and RPGs. At first light the next morning the Australians swept the area, wading through the shallow river at low tide, subsequently locating another damaged sampan, an AK-47, an RPG-2 and two RPG rounds.

On 16 February, just prior to a cease-fire for the Tet New Year festival, the Australians had received information from an agent about the location of large weapon caches in the north of AO Tiki, and a large Viet Cong was also expected to be in position. B and W Companies 4RAR/NZ, each accompanied by a tracker team and a Centurion tank troop from B Squadron, 1st Armoured Regiment were subsequently tasked to patrol to the area by separate routes. Accompanied by the Hoi Chanh, B Company—under the command of Major Bill Reynolds—crossed an open area during the early afternoon and moved into some dense vegetation, patrolling up to an occupied communist position unaware. Well concealed in bunkers the Viet Cong successfully initiated a command-detonated directional mine and opened fire with small-arms and RPGs, inflicting a number of casualties on the Australians, including one killed and five wounded. In response the Australian tanks—under the command of Second Lieutenant Brian Sullivan—moved forward to support the infantry, and in the ensuring battle two were damaged, including one which was knocked out by a rocket propelled grenade which penetrated the turret and inflicted severe injuries on the crew. Yet under the leadership of Reynolds, B Company fought to regain its balance following the initial onslaught, and was able to withdraw under the fire of the surviving tanks which engaged the bunkers at point-blank with their 20 pounder main armament, using solid shot and canister anti-personnel rounds which stripped the undergrowth. The Australian casualties were moved back to safety by stretcher bearers who had moved forward under covering fire, and the damaged tank was also successfully recovered.

Meanwhile the 4RAR/NZ Regimental Medical Officer, Captain Dave Lewis had commandeered a Bell H-13 Sioux light observation helicopters from 161 Reconnaissance Flight and flew in to assist the treatment of the casualties. Despite his efforts however, one of the most badly injured soldiers succumbed to his wounds. The remainder of the casualties were then moved by helicopter to the Australian Field Hospital at Vung Tau. The Australians then called-in artillery fire which was adjusted onto the bunker system, with the 105 mm guns of 104 Field Battery being augmented by those of 102 Field Battery in the neighbouring AO, and American 155 mm self propelled guns. A number of air strikes were also directed onto the position, while Reynolds planned an attack to destroy the Viet

Cong force. Gradually B Company gained the upper hand and prepared to assault the position, returning heavy fire with small arms while the tanks continued to engage the bunkers from close range. The contact had continued until late afternoon, however with the truce due to come into effect for Tet, American fire support would cease to be available at 17:00, after which a 24-hour cease-fire would commence. Circling overhead in another Sioux helicopter Greville protested, and although Pearson had supported him the Americans refused to provide offensive support despite the contact having been initiated by the Viet Cong. Reynolds could continue the assault if he wished, but he would only have the limited fire support from the two tanks capable of firing and the Australian field artillery, while the battalion mortars were out of range and would have been inadequate nonetheless.

Lacking the medium artillery and air strikes required to successfully assault the fortified position, B Company withdrew to a safe distance and kept the position under observation and fire. Meanwhile a follow-up attack schedule for the next day was also cancelled due to the unavailability of American artillery. During the night a large Viet Cong force was observed withdrawing, with one party of about 30 men passing close to a concealed Centurion; frustrated, the Australians observed the truce and held their fire. The next morning, 17 January, with the area now stripped bare of vegetation the devastation caused to the bunker system was obvious and it was clear that the position had been hit heavily by the Australian tanks and artillery. Although there were numerous signs of casualties, with a large number of blood trails and some damaged weapons the Australians found only three dead, with the Viet Cong once again having cleared the battlefield of the dead and wounded during the night. Later intelligence suggested that the position had been occupied by the headquarters of 274 VC Regiment and one of its battalions and the Australians considered it likely that the Viet Cong battalion had fought a delaying action in order to allow the headquarters to withdraw, before itself retiring under cover of darkness. A thorough search of the area by the Australians was not possible however, and B Company was ordered to return to their patrol area in order to prepare for redeployment. The fighting had been one of the more significant actions of Operation Goodwood and for his leadership during this action Reynolds was awarded the Military Cross. Corporal Wayne Brown—the B Company Medical Assistant—was awarded the Military Medal, while Sullivan and Brett were both Mentioned in Despatches.

Operation Goodwood concludes, 17–19 February 1969

Just after dusk on 17 January, following the end of the Tet truce, a large communist force attacked a South Vietnamese post across the river on 4RAR/NZs western boundary, before withdrawing back along a creek towards FSB Janice. At 01:45 on 18 February a sentry from D Company had detected noise and movement to the south, just outside the wire. Estimated at up to company strength, the Viet Cong were observed clearly through a Starlight scope and were moving noisily, likely unaware of their proximity to the fire support base. Meanwhile the mortar fire controller (MFC) had moved to the sentry position, and as the Viet Cong force commenced crossing the creek they were engaged by the Australians with more than 100 rounds of mortar fire at a range of just 200 metres (220 yd) from the base plate location. The initial bombardment caused confusion among the Viet Cong and they took no evasive action, instead continuing to attempt to cross the creek. Several more rounds then landed among them, causing numerous casualties and forcing the survivors to withdraw. As with previous contacts, the Viet Cong once again demonstrated their skill in removing their casualties from the battlefield and clearing patrols sent out at first light by the Australians found no bodies, although numerous blood trails and drag marks were observed indicating that the Viet Cong had suffered heavily. A large quantity of discarded weapons, equipment and ammunition was captured by the Australians however, including seven AK-47s, four RPG-2s, an L1A1 Self Loading Rifle, a pistol, a 12.7 mm heavy machine-gun and armour piercing rounds.

Meanwhile, 9RAR had continued to maintain its blocking operations, however on 16 February it was redeployed to AO Belconnen in order to shield the American bases at Long Binh and Bien Hoa against attacks expected during Tet as part of a new operation, known as Operation Federal. Later, in response to the upcoming communist offensive Pearson also warned Greville to be prepared to move 4RAR/NZ further north to help defend Long Binh and Bien Hoa. With the Australians having penetrated into the heart of a major Viet Cong sanctuary, it was likely that the Viet Cong had left a large number of caches in the area after being forced to withdraw, however time would not permit 4RAR/NZ to conduct a thorough search of the area. Yet even as the operation was winding down V Company 4RAR/NZ had a number of successful contacts in AO Riverdale over the next two days, killing at least two Viet Cong in two separate incidents on 18 and 19 February.

Aftermath

After 78 days Operation Goodwood concluded on 19 February 1969. FSB Julia closed and HQ 1ATF moved to FSB Kerry in preparation for upcoming operations. Australian casualties included 21 killed and 91 wounded, while allied casualties included 31 South Vietnamese killed and 81 wounded, as well as 7 Americans wounded. Meanwhile, North Vietnamese and Viet Cong losses amounted to at least 245 killed, 39 possibly killed, 45 wounded and 17 captured, during 274 separate contacts. Nearly 2,000 bunkers were uncovered and many destroyed, while more than 280 rocket propelled grenades, 70 anti-personnel mines, 490 grenades and 450 pounds of explosives were captured. Throughout the operation the bulk of the contacts had been initiated by the Australians, a reverse of the American trend in which more than two-thirds of actions were normally initiated by the Viet Cong. Although there were few major actions, the operation was considered a success by the Australians and following it Viet Cong activity in 1ATFs area of operations visibly lessened as the communists were forced to abandon their permanent bases in the Hat Dich, and disrupting their preparations for upcoming offensive operations. Operation Goodwood was one of the longest out of province operations mounted by the Australians during the war and was also the last Australian multi-battalion operation to be fought across the border with third-country forces. From 1969 most operations tended to be platoon and company-sized, and confined to Phuoc Tuy. It had been a period of intense activity for the Australians and the Royal Australian Regiment, the 3rd Cavalry Regiment and 1st Armoured Regiment were subsequently awarded the battle honour 'Hat Dich', one of only five awarded to Australian units during the war.

There was little respite for the Australians though, with both 4RAR/NZ and 9RAR immediately redeploying in anticipation of another communist offensive during Tet, under Operation Federal. This operation in late-February 1969 saw 1ATF—less one battalion and other elements required to secure its base in Nui Dat—once again operating outside Phuoc Tuy province to secure the major bases of Long Binh, Bien Hoa and the capital Saigon from an impending offensive. However, unlike the previous two episodes—Operation Coburg in January and February 1968, and Operation Thoan Thang I in May 1968 which had both involved large-scale attacks on the Australian positions, Operational Federal was less intensive and was limited to ambushing and patrolling, with none of the Australian fire support bases subjected to attack. 1RAR subsequently returned to Australia after being relieved by 5RAR—under the command of Lieutenant Colonel Colin Kahn—on 15 February. Arriving in Sydney on 28 February 1969, 1RAR was welcomed home with a march through the city. During the tour—its second in Vietnam—the battalion had killed at least 276 Viet Cong and destroyed a large number of bunkers, camps, and caches and had been heavily involved in the Battle of Coral-Balmoral. 1RARs own casualties had been high however, losing 31 killed and 165 wounded.

The communist 1969 Tet offensive began in the early hours of 23 February, with attacks against US and ARVN installations and district capitals. Lacking the ferocity of the offensive in 1968, the outburst soon slackened, however. In III CTZ, where 1ATF operated, over a period of five days there were 175 attacks by fire and just 15 ground assaults, while the communists suffered over 1,800 killed and 320 captured. Indeed for the Australians the offensive proved to be only a series of relatively minor disturbances when compared to that of the year before; perhaps demoralised following the earlier mauling at Coral and Balmoral the Viet Cong declined to attack major South Vietnamese and US installations in force. Regardless, with the bulk of 1ATF operating away from Nui Dat in first half of 1969, the Viet Cong again became active in the populated central and southern areas of Phuoc Tuy Province, including Dat Do and Long Dien, and the villages between Dat Do and the coast. Although ARVN forces were by now operating in these areas, communist guerrilla groups operated with freedom, especially at night. As a consequence Australian operations in mid-1969 were forced to focus on the area around Dat Do and the Long Hai Hills, as they attempted to restrict the Viet Cong's access to the local population. Later, on 6–7 June 1969 the Australians were engaged in fierce close-quarter house-to-house fighting during the Battle of Binh Ba.

Source (edited): "http://en.wikipedia.org/wiki/Battle_of_Hat_Dich"

Battle of Lima Site 85

The **Battle of Lima Site 85**, also called **Battle of Phou Pha Thi**, was a battle of the Vietnam War that resulted in the largest single ground combat loss of United States Air Force members in that war. The site was located atop Phou Pha Thi; a mountain in Viengxay District, Houaphanh Province, Laos, 15 miles (24 km) from the border of the Democratic Republic of Vietnam (DRV or North Vietnam) and 30 miles (48 km) from Sam Neua, capital of the Pathet Lao.

Background

The term "Lima Site" was derived from the American acronym for map designations of "Landing Sites" within the Secret War zone of the Second Indochina War, an active though covert battleground in the larger Cold War. Because Laos was considered a neutral country by the International Agreement on the Neutrality of Laos signed in Geneva, Switzerland on 23 July 1962 by 14 nations (including the People's Republic of China, the Soviet Union, North and South Vietnam and the United States,) existence of these sites was not officially acknowledged until 1986. At the time of the battle, radar technicians whose parent unit was the 1st Combat Evaluation Group (1CEVG) manned LS-85. Like Raven Forward Air Controllerss, they had been temporarily discharged from the military in a process called "sheep-dipping," The technicians had no training in close quarters combat as there were plans in place to evacuate them before it came to that, but they remained on the mountain one day too long.

In August 1966, the United States Air Force sited a TACAN facility on the peak of Phu Pha Thi to assist American aviators conducting bombing operations in the northwestern region of North Vietnam. In 1967, a COMBAT

SKYSPOT ground directed bombing system, the AN/TSQ 81 (portable version of the AN/MSQ-77 Radar Bombing Control System) was added in a mission with the code name "HEAVY GREEN" and was operational by the end of November with code name "COMMANDO CLUB". The COMMANDO CLUB mission was to provide radar information and assistance to U.S. aircraft bombing military targets in Hanoi, Vietnam and its surrounding areas in Operation Rolling Thunder, and along the Ho Chi Minh Trail in Operation Barrel Roll. From November through 20 March 1968, the site directed 99 of 427 Operation Rolling Thunder strike missions, slightly over 23% of the total. Throughout this period, 1,472 strike missions were flown into Operation Barrel Roll; 408 or 27.7% were directed by Site 85. From 1–10 March, the site directed 165 of 182 sorties in self-defense.

Aerial attack

On 12 January 1968, four Vietnam People's Air Force Antonov An-2 (NATO reporting name "Colt") biplanes lifted off on a mission to destroy the base. The Antonovs reached LS 85 and two Antonovs began dropping 120-mm mortar rounds on the site and making strafing runs.

"An Air Combat First" - CIA painting of Air America helicopter engaging 2 VPAF AN-2 biplanes

An Air America Bell 205 helicopter, carrying ammunition to the site, lifted off to avoid destruction. Captain Ted Moore said that the attack "Looked like World War I," and gave chase to a Antonov as it turned back to the Vietnamese border. Moore positioned his helicopter above the biplane, as Crew Chief Glenn Woods fired an AK-47 rifle down on it. The pursuit continued for more than 20 minutes until the second AN-2 flew underneath the helicopter. Moore and Woods watched as the first AN-2 dropped and crashed into a ridge just west of the North Vietnamese border. The second Antonov hit the side of a mountain 5 km farther north. The other Antonovs escaped, inactive observers throughout. Within hours a CIA Special Activities Division team reached the crashed aircraft and found bullet holes in the downed planes.

Ted Moore and Glenn Woods gained the distinction of having shot down a fixed-wing aircraft from a helicopter, a singular aerial victory in the Vietnam War. On 27 July 2007, the CIA officially dedicated a painting entitled "An Air Combat First" in an event attended by members of the Air America Board; pilot Ted Moore; Sawang Reed, the wife of flight mechanic Glenn Woods; CIA paramilitary legend Bill Lair; and the donors of the painting, former Air America officers Marius Burke and Boyd D. Mesecher. The Vietnam People's Air Force Museum, Hanoi has on display an Antonov used in the attack.

Ground Battle

The configuration of Lima Site 85.

By 10 March the opposition was ready for another attack, this time utilizing the 41st *Dac Cong* (sapper) Battalion of the People's Army of Vietnam (PAVN) and the 923rd PAVN Infantry Battalion, which had the task of capturing or destroying the radar equipment and covert USAF personnel at LS-85.

On the night of 10 March the 766th PAVN Regiment launched a diversionary attack preceded by an artillery barrage. Lima Site 85 was encircled by the North Vietnamese to trap the American personnel there, while all egress routes were blocked to prevent rescue by Thai paramilitary "volunteers" and Royal Lao Army Hmong paramilitary. During the night, heavily-armed infiltrators scaled the 5,600-foot (1,700 m) mountain, while PAVN infantry units fought their way up the slopes to create a diversion. The Americans were taken by surprise when 33 sappers appeared with submachine guns and RPG-7s.

Throughout the night, U.S. F-4 Phantom fighter-bombers and A-26 bombers repeatedly hit the attackers, while simultaneously, Air America aircraft were ready to evacuate the survivors. Five men took cover on a ledge 10 to 15 feet below the top of the hill with a nearly 3,000-foot straight drop below, where they were effectively trapped. Following an exchange of small-arms fire and grenades, two were wounded, two dead, and the body of one of them rolled over on top of a grenade that had landed nearby, but out of reach. Richard Etchberger, the one not wounded, tended to the others and fought off the advancing North Vietnamese troops until a rescue helicopter arrived. He then helped load the wounded onto slings to be lifted into the hovering aircraft before coming aboard himself. As the helicopter headed towards an air base in Thailand, an enemy soldier fired upon the aircraft, fatally wounding Etchberger. By morning, USAF and Air America missions had airlifted out the surviving defenders from the top of the mountain, the Hmong and Thai troops abandoned the base of the mountain and Lima Site 85 fell to communist forces.

Aftermath

Once the 41st PAVN Sapper Battalion had secured the site, its members began collecting the TSQ 81 equipment and documents. It was assumed that North Vietnamese soldiers buried the dead Americans or that their remains had been destroyed during air strikes on the base; no claim of POWs was made by the North Vietnamese.

Two days after the fall of Lima Site

85, Captain Donald Elliot Westbrook's A-1 Skyraider was shot down while searching for possible survivors.

On 18 July 1968 with heavy air support from the CIA and Air Force, a few of Vang Pao's Hmong commandos managed to reach the destroyed helipad and TSQ facility, but they were unable to hold the ridgeline. The 148th PAVN Regiment sent Vang Pao's troops reeling with heavy casualties.

Eleven of the twelve Americans lost the day of the battle were listed first as missing in action (MIA), then later as KIA/body not recovered. A further 42 soldiers of the Thai "volunteers" and of General Vang Pao's Hmong paramilitary were killed during the action. Because of the secrecy of the mission, and the US government's desire for plausible deniability, Etchberger and fellow technicians who operated the radar site were actually discharged from the Air Force and made into Lockheed Corporation employees prior to beginning the mission; the Air Force posthumously accepted Chief Master Sergeant Etchberger back into the Air Force and award him medals for his gallantry. Although recommended for the Medal of Honor shortly after his death, President Lyndon B. Johnson rejected the nomination because the Lima Site mission was classified at the time.

Pentagon officials told Cory Etchberger that his father died in a helicopter accident in Southeast Asia on March 11, 1968. But even at 9 years old, Cory said he felt something was missing in the story when his family was secretly whisked into the Pentagon to accept his father's Air Force Cross.

After the Lima Site mission had been declassified in 1983, veterans of the 1CEVG began requesting that Etchberger's Air Force Cross be upgraded. This was approved by Secretary of the Air Force Michael B. Donley in 2008, and by Congress in 2009. President Barack Obama formally awarded the Medal of Honor at the White House Tuesday, September 21, 2010.

A formerly TOP SECRET AIR FORCE EYES ONLY LIMITED DISTRIBUTION after-action report dated 9 August 1968 is now de-classified.

USAF personnel at Phou Pha Thi (Lima Site 85) on 11 March 1968

The patch of the 1st AACS Mobile Communications Group present at Lima Site 85.

- Rescued: Capt Stanley J. Sliz, SSgt John Daniel, SSgt Bill Husband, SSgt Jack Starling, Sgt Roger Huffman, Howard Freeman (CIA), John Spence (CIA)
- KIA during rescue: CMSgt Richard L. Etchberger, posthumously awarded the Medal of Honor in 2010.
- MIA later changed to KIA/body not recovered: Lt Col Clarence F. Blanton, MSgt James H. Calfee, TSgt Melvin A. Holland, SSgt Herbert A. Kirk, SSgt Henry G. Gish, SSgt Willis R. Hall, SSgt James W. Davis, SSgt David S. Price, TSgt Donald K. Springsteadah, SSgt Don F. Worley
- MIA later changed to KIA/body not recovered later changed to KIA/remains recovered: TSgt Patrick L. Shannon

Memorials to CombatSpot and Arc Light airmen are co-located on Andersen Air Force Base, Guam.

Search and recovery of remains at LS-85

Between 1994 and 2004, 11 investigations were conducted by both Joint POW/MIA Accounting Command (JPAC) and unilaterally by Lao and Vietnamese investigators on both sides of the border.

In 2002 two of the PAVN soldiers who had taken part in the attack told investigators that they threw the bodies of the Americans off the mountain after the attack as they were unable to bury them on the rocky surface.

In March 2003, JPAC investigators threw dummies over the edge at those points indicated by the PAVN soldiers while a photographer in a helicopter videotaped their fall. That pointed the investigators to a ledge, 540 feet below. Several mountaineer-qualified JPAC specialists scaled down the cliffs to the ledge where they recovered leather boots in four different sizes, five survival vests, and other fragments of material that indicated the presence of at least four Americans.

On 7 December 2005 the Defense Prisoner of War/Missing Personnel Office announced that the remains of TSgt Patrick L. Shannon had been identified and were being returned to his family.

On 14 February 2007 the remains of Captain Donald Westbrook, who had been shot down in 1968 while searching for possible survivors of the Battle of Lima Site 85, were positively identified from remains which had been returned in September 1998.

Source (edited): "http://en.wikipedia.org/wiki/Battle_of_Lima_Site_85"